Coping FOR KIDS

A Complete Stress-Control Program for Students Ages 8-18

by Gerald Herzfeld, Ph.D.
& Robin Powell, Ph.D.

illustrated by Sylvie Seguin and Robin Powell

THE CENTER FOR APPLIED RESEARCH IN EDUCATION, INC.
West Nyack, New York 10994

The procedures and suggestions contained in this book are not intended as substitutes for consultation with a licensed physician. The methods discussed in these pages may not be appropriate for some children with physical problems. If a child has known medical problems, particularly epilepsy or diabetes, consult with the child's physician before administering these techniques. All matters regarding a child's health require medical supervision; if in doubt, ask a doctor for advice.

10   9   8   7   6

Cover Photo Credit: Paula Court

ISBN 0-87628-233-8   OVERALL PACKAGE

ISBN 0-87628-234-6   TEACHER'S MANUAL

ISBN 0-87628-235-4   TAPE 1

ISBN 0-87628-236-2   TAPE 2

ISBN 0-87628-237-8   WORKBOOK

PRINTED IN THE UNITED STATES OF AMERICA

This book is dedicated to my mother, Evelyn Herzfeld, and to the memory of my father, Paul A. Herzfeld

Special thanks to:

Dr. Edward Taub, whose generosity and guidance enabled me to get started in this field;

Debra Chez, whose encouragement and patience enabled me to finish this project;

Gregory Harrison, for his expert work on the production of the cassette portion of this program;

Steven Baker, for the original music composition on the cassettes;

Kristen Cywinski, Mark Gilroy Wisniewski, Donna Steffen, Vincent Pastina, Siobhan Rohan, and Michael J. Cunningham, for narrating the introductory cassette.

About the Authors

Gerald Herzfeld, Ph.D., is a psychologist in clinical practice in biofeedback, stress management, and relaxation training. He also is a remedial reading specialist with 14 years of classroom teaching experience in grades 3 to 6. Dr. Herzfeld has more than 10 years of experience in biofeedback, including work for the Institute for Behavioral Research in Washington, D.C., and research with Dr. Edward Taub, past president of the Biofeedback Society of America. His research has been presented to state and national meetings of the Biofeedback Society of America and has been published in professional journals.

Robin Powell, Ph.D., is a movement therapist in private practice. She also teaches body awareness, corrective fitness, and stress management, and has taught at the State University College at Buffalo (New York). Dr. Powell teaches continuing education classes for adults at several institutions, including New York University. With a background in dance, physical education, and movement therapy, Dr. Powell is a certified kinetic awareness teacher and has studied and written on Ideokinesis, Alexander, and Feldenkrais techniques. She has trained in stress management with Dr. Norman Shealy at the Shealy Pain and Stress Rehabilitation Institute.

About This Program

Coping for Kids offers teachers, guidance counselors, school psychologists, and other professional educators a step-by-step program of techniques, exercises, and activities for teaching children ages 8–18 how to control their own stress. Once students can do this, they become calmer, more receptive to learning, and easier to teach.

With society's emphasis on success, stress can begin at a very early age and continue throughout a person's life. Every day, stressful situations at home and in school can place great demands on a young person's body and mind, which in turn can cause physical reactions that can become lifelong habits. These reactions can be undesirable and impair performance. They may even lead to the development of physical symptoms or serious illness later on in life.

Coping for Kids helps children and teenagers learn to relax and overcome their stresses by using the 28 ready-to-use lessons and over 45 reproducible activity worksheets that appear both in this book and in a separate workbook available from the publisher. An important feature of this stress-control program is the eight short lessons on the two cassette tapes that help students learn to relax, breathe properly, and become aware of their own body movements. Each taped lesson's complete dialogue is printed in this book.

These techniques and activities provide the following benefits to your students:

- They teach children about stress and how it can affect them.
- They show children that their experiences are usually shared by others and that they are not alone in facing them.

- They offer children alternatives to the usual harmful reactions to stress, both behaviorally and physiologically.
- They help children recognize their own habitual muscle tension and teach them how to eliminate it.

This program is intended to prepare you to work effectively with children to manage their stress. Background information is included with each of the 28 lessons to help you understand fully each relaxation technique and stress control topic. Each background section is followed by a lesson that states the purpose, materials needed, step-by-step procedures, and follow-up suggestions, as well as which audio tape to play for your students. You may use as much or as little of the material as you feel is necessary for yourself and your students. The goal is to teach children these relaxation techniques so they can begin using them whenever and wherever they feel stressed. Stress may be caused by

- Test anxiety
- "Stage fright" before speeches
- Nervousness about competition and tryouts
- Peer pressure
- Concerns about self-concept and appearance
- Family problems
- Self-consciousness and lack of confidence during adolescence
- Pressures of our fast-paced world

While it would be unrealistic to guarantee that all your students will be completely relieved of stress and of all their problems simply by using this program, you can be instrumental in helping them learn how to cope with stress—now and for a lifetime.

Gerald Herzfeld

Robin Powell

Contents

LESSON 19: Making Friends and Developing Confidants • *144*

LESSON 20: Creative Problem Solving • *149*

LESSON 21: Expressing Emotions • *155*

LESSON 22: Improving Self-Esteem • *161*

LESSON 23: Developing Coping Phrases • *165*

LESSON 1

What Is Stress?

BACKGROUND FOR THE TEACHER

Stress can be defined simply as the body's nonspecific response to the demands made on it. Stress is a result, so something can produce stress without actually *being* stress. For example, anger, pain, and embarrassment can cause stress, but they are not stress itself. Something that causes stress is called a *stressor.*

Stress can be caused by a positive as well as a negative stimulus; the same nonspecific response of the body to adjust to the situation may result from either. For example, a person who wins a large sum of money in a lottery will experience stress. There may be a similar reaction in a negative situation if the same person discovers he cannot find his winning ticket, and he can suffer the same stress reaction once again when he finds the winning ticket.

Stress can mean different things to different people. Virtually anything can cause a stressful reaction in someone, since situations that are not stressful to one person may cause another to feel very stressed. Similarly, an event that causes a person to experience stress one day may not even be noticed the next day, depending on circumstances, the individual's mood, and so on. A specific situation may be a stressor, and the exact opposite situation may also cause stress. An example of this would be giving someone too much or too little responsibility, both of which can result in stress. Genetic factors, the differences in people's personalities, in their tolerance for ambiguity, in their ability to cope with change, and in their motivation, can affect individual reactions to particular stressors.

What Happens to the Body Under Stress

In stressful situations, we experience what scientist Hans Selye calls the *General Adaptation Syndrome. (The Stress of Life,* 1956) This is the body's total mobilization to cope with stress. Dr. Walter Cannon identified the body's immediate reaction to a threatening situation as the "fight or flight" response. This occurs when the body "moves into gear" for its immediate response. It is something like revving up a race car at the starting line—it is already operating at a high level when it takes off. There is an immediate surge of energy, adrenaline is secreted, respiration increases, muscles tense and prepare for action, and the heart rate and blood pressure increase as more blood is pumped and more energy is made available. Sugar production and its secretion into the blood is increased as well. The skin capillaries and other blood vessels constrict. Digestion is slowed, allowing energy to be used elsewhere.

All these reactions were critical to survival in the early evolution of man, so that he could respond quickly to situations that demanded action, such as fighting or running away. Decisions had to be made very quickly, and physical changes had to occur rapidly as well, for hesitation could be fatal. This physiological reaction is still present in man. The General Adaptation Syndrome is a total reaction. Selye characterized it by three stages. The first stage is alarm, whereby the body mobilizes for action. The second stage is resistance, whereby the part of the body or system attacked (or designated as best able to deal with the situation) takes action. The third stage is exhaustion, which occurs as resistance wears down. This last stage is a reaction to the first two and can allow for recovery or for the first stage to recur. When an individual continually responds to stress in this manner, the body is weakened and becomes susceptible to illness and disease. Thus stress and illness are inextricably intertwined.

The body's natural tendency is to return to a normal, healthy level of functioning. This is called *homeostasis,* the action of which has been likened to that of a thermostat. Within homeostasis there is an acceptable range of functioning. If an individual begins to function outside this range, the body takes action to bring it within acceptable boundaries.

A problem exists when children and adults learn to override this mechanism. They can learn to respond with a "fight or flight" response, then go through the course of the General Adaptation Syndrome as a result of a large variety of life situations, even though these situations may not really call for such extreme reactions and physiological changes. When we hear a story of how a mother somehow found great strength to save her endangered child, we see how an emergency situation can cause a beneficial physiological change. However, it is not necessary for the body to respond with such drastic changes for every slightly stressful situation.

For example, many teachers and students have felt their bodies react with stress when the principal walked into the room. When a test is being given, when a child is called on to give an answer, and in a hundred other situations, there may be physiological reactions that increase the body's arousal level even though these are not needed in these situations and may even be detrimental. The stress reaction may impair performance in these situations, and the physiological reactions may make it harder for us to respond appropriately.

Because of the physiological changes caused by the stress response, both children and adults may often function at an elevated level of arousal and for an unnecessarily long period of time. If we react to these stressors but then fail to turn off the reaction, we may never return to safe, resting levels of arousal and may eventually override the homeostatic mechanism. Even when we are able to return to a lower level of arousal, we may not do it as rapidly as we should, and can operate for too long a period of time at the elevated arousal level.

Try to visualize it this way: We start off at a low optimum, arousal level, which can be represented as zero. The presence of a stressor then raises the arousal level to 20. The person deals with the stressor and begins to return to zero. Another stressor impinges on the person, however, and the level, which has lowered to 10, now rises to 30. This pattern may continue throughout the day, with the level never again reaching zero. Prolonged occurrences of stressful situations may cause the arousal level to be constantly elevated so that the person's normal level of arousal is now somewhat higher than "zero" or optimal level. The person then is functioning in a weakened state. The muscles can be overloaded, the emotions may be strained, the immune system may not function at a peak level, and exhaustion can result. Other stress-related illnesses may occur, such as ulcers, diarrhea, constipation, cholesterol irregularities, colitis, gastritis, poor appetite, cardiovascular problems, heart attacks, headaches, abnormal blood pressure, asthma, low resistance to disease, skin problems, and sleep problems. Smoking, drinking and taking drugs may also result from stress.

Although children may or may not yet be exhibiting these symptoms, they can be well on their way to manifesting them. Children who are experiencing stress may have difficulty concentrating, get poor grades in school, have trouble interacting, be hyperactive, and so on. The most likely physical manifestations are headaches, stomach troubles, susceptibility to illness, teeth grinding, and facial tics. Aggressiveness, daydreaming, school phobias, and school burnout may also occur in children because of stress. Some may withdraw and become loners or nonparticipants, some turn to gangs or cults for security, and some turn to alcohol or drugs to escape from stressful feelings. In some instances, suicide is the action taken as a result of stress.

Once a child or adult gets into these habits, they are difficult to change. People do not just relax because they are told to do so, and many people have lost the ability to turn off or reverse the stress reaction. They may be unaware that they are holding tension in their muscles, for example, until a symptom results because of the overload on that part of the body. In addition, even a person who feels that he or she is taking time and relaxing may not actually be lowering his or her arousal level during these periods.

Children often see adults resorting to tranquilizers and alcohol to cope with stress. They need to learn that there are better alternatives—simple relaxation techniques that can be used to keep the body calm and to recover quickly from stress reactions.

After they have used the techniques from this program a number of times, the children's bodies should begin to react automatically and less harmfully to stressful situations. That is to say, by pairing stressful situations with relaxation enough times, we may begin to get an association between the two so that the body reacts to the stressful situation by returning to a calm level immediately. We will not be able to prevent a reaction to stress, and may not even want to, but we can bring a quick recovery from it.

LESSON 1

Purpose: To introduce the children to the idea of stress and to define some of the terms used to refer to stress.

Materials Needed

    Workbook Activity 1-1

Directions

    1. Read the introduction to Activity 1-1 as the children follow along in their workbook.

    2. Discuss the following questions and answers:

- What is the difference between *stress* and a *stressor? (A stressor* causes stress. *Stress* is the reaction of the person to the stressor.)

- What is *homeostasis? (Homeostasis* is the body's tendency to return itself to a good level of functioning.)

- Explain the *fight or flight* response and tell about a few of the things that happen to your body when it occurs. (The *fight or flight* response is the body's reaction to a stressful situation. There are physiological changes, such as an increase in sugar sent into the blood, vasoconstriction, slowed digestion, secretion of adrenaline, increased muscle tension, changes in breathing, and sweating.)

- What is a *symptom?* (A *symptom* is a condition that develops in the body as a result of a problem.)

Stress

DIRECTIONS: Follow along with your teacher as this introduction to stress is read. Be prepared to answer the questions your teacher will ask.

Stress is your reaction to something that happens. It is what you feel. Since it is how *you* react to something, and not everybody will be bothered by that same thing, it must be *your* inner feeling. For example, John gets upset by being told what to do. Mark prefers it so that he doesn't have to worry about making decisions. Being told what to do does not cause stress then. If it did, Mark would be affected by it too. But John does suffer stress from it; stress is what he feels inside. It shows in things that happen to his body and in his mind.

We call something that causes stress a *stressor.* Being told what to do is a stressor for John, but not for Mark. John may like to make decisions. Mark doesn't. Making decisions, then, is a stressor for Mark but not for John. Everybody has his or her own stressors that affect them.

Everybody comes across situations that can cause them to feel stress at home, in school, and on their jobs.

What Happens Under Stress

When you suffer from stress you may not be able to perform as well as you normally would. Changes occur in your body, and these may prevent you from doing as well as you might. Your body can react to a stressor with what is called the "fight or flight" response. It's kind of like when you've seen pictures showing a race car driver "give it the gas" and shoot forward with a surge of energy at the start of a race, or when Popeye has his spinach. Your body has many physical reactions. You get extra energy because extra sugar is sent into the blood and other body functions, like digestion, slow down, so that the energy can be used where you need it most. Something called *vasoconstriction* occurs, which is where the blood vessels constrict so that less blood gets to the extremities (that's why your hands get cold—there is less blood there). Certain hormones, such as adrenaline, are sent into the bloodstream. This makes your muscles tighten and your breathing change. You may even sweat.

In emergency situations, these can be very helpful because they make your body ready to react quickly. It is not good to have your body go through all of these changes for every little stressor that you experience, however. It's like revving up a car; you wouldn't want to do it all the time because it would burn the engine out. There can be a problem if people have this reaction too often, or if they don't get themselves back down to a calm level.

Usually the body will try to return to a calm level on its own. There is a word for the way the body gets itself back to a normal, calmer level of functioning, called *homeostasis.* Our body's homeostatic mechanism works in the same way as a thermostat—it shuts itself off and turns itself on in order to stay at the right level. When stressors act on a person, and that person has this "fight or flight" response too often, the person may learn to override the homeostatic mechanism and train his or her body to stay at a high level. This is unhealthy because at some point some part of the body gets overloaded and a *symptom* of too much stress will develop, such as a headache, stomach trouble, muscle pain, and so on.

Kids' Stressors

BACKGROUND FOR THE TEACHER

This introductory tape presents a number of examples of stressful situations that children may encounter. Although this is only a sample rather than a complete list of these kinds of situations, every child should be able to find something here with which to identify.

Of course every child has unique experiences and individual reactions to situations. A pleasant situation to one child may be stressful to another, and vice versa. It is our hope that the children will see that their reactions are not abnormal, will also begin to realize that they are not powerless in these situations, and will learn that they do not have to be affected so strongly by them.

A more thorough background of the kinds of stresses children encounter is presented here and on the tape so that the teacher (parent, therapist, etc.) may be more sensitive to what children are exposed to and experience as a result.

Parental Influence

It is not very long after birth that pressure is first put on children. We live in a fast-paced, achievement-oriented society. For whatever reasons, such as competitiveness, status, insecurity, laziness, advice from so-called experts, and so on, parents tend to put pressure on infants to walk, to talk, and be toilet trained at an early age. In spite of our present knowledge that development is not the same in all children, nor is early development an indication of later success, many parents still take great pride in hearing people respond to their child's early progress with comments like, "Isn't she smart." These same parents would dread hearing comments such as, "You mean she doesn't talk yet?"

Many educators and other professionals have in recent years indicated that if teaching isn't begun at an early age, golden opportunity is being missed. This had led to early teaching at home and to children's being enrolled in preschool programs when very young. There is pressure put on preschool children to learn to count and to memorize the alphabet, among other things. Parents may begin this pressure, but educational TV programming for children has increased their pressures. When the neighbor's children learn to count by watching children's TV programs, a child may be introduced at a very early age to stress caused by competitiveness.

Children can be labeled "losers," "slow," "emotionally immature," and so on if they do not achieve success early. These labels create behaviors in children and in those with whom they interact, thus becoming an early source of pressure and stress. It seems that we no longer want to wait for the late bloomers to bloom. Many parents, for that matter, will not allow retention in a grade for fear of being embarrassed that their child has failed.

Adults have a great deal of job dissatisfaction as well as feelings of failure these days, so many try to live through their children, thus burdening them with extra pressures. The push for success may not be in the child's best interest, but rather may be done to increase the parents' self-esteem. Parents who want to show others that they are concerned parents may use their children as status symbols as well. Mothers may have given up careers or made other sacrifices in order to have children, so they put pressure on their children to succeed to assure themselves that giving up their former lifestyle was worth it.

Along with the early pressure to achieve academic success, other developments have also cut into a formerly carefree childhood and have accelerated the process of growing up. For example, the style of dress has changed. Rather than children wearing "children's clothes" as in past generations, children are now often carbon copies of adults. There is also more pressure these days to discover something in which the child excels and then to encourage the child to devote great amounts of time to cultivating that skill. Illustrations of this are early piano lessons, dance lessons, specialized computer or sports camps, organized sports for young children, and so on. It seems that we no longer allow children to waste time having fun, or being carefree and unconcerned about the future.

The Media

We have become a media-oriented society, and television is an important part of most children's lives. This alone may have accelerated the pace of this generation's growth and increased the amount of stress to which they are exposed. Television programs and movies portray children as looking and acting grown up, wearing adult clothes, and having grownup feelings and problems. They behave as grownups do and use adult strategies in their relationships. The problem with this is that it can change children's ideas about what is a normal way for them to behave; they cannot help comparing themselves to these children on the screen.

Any television show demands the absorption of a lot of facts in a short period of time. The viewer is assaulted with conversations, plot developments, and so on, which must be absorbed, catalogued, and applied to what he or she already knows about the show's content in order to keep up. This requires that the child use high-order thinking skills, such as inference, drawing conclusions, and predicting outcomes.

The media have also made it possible for children as well as adults to be aware, almost instantaneously, of ominous events all over the world. We are thus able to worry about events all over the world, not just at home. The nuclear age and the threat of world destruction, make all our lives even more stressful.

The advertising industry realizes that children are a profitable market, and commercials urge children to do all sorts of grownup things and to make grownup-type decisions. Commercials may even push adult products on children, such as makeup for little girls. This can also contribute to the trend of early adolescence.

Adult subjects are now also fashionable in children's books, which are increasingly looking for "realism." The same holds true in magazines for the younger reader, which now have more adult themes.

Early Exposure to Sex

Studies indicate that there are instances of early sex and early pregnancy now more than ever.

Sexual themes are increasingly more available to be seen by children in movies, in cable and broadcast television, and in the lyrics of rock music. There has been a trend toward sexual experience at a younger age for a number of years. The media's portrayal of young people in sexual situations may have had some effect on this.

Sex education in the schools is another new development that may have affected the earlier maturation of children. In addition, the changing nature of people's relationships and of families in general has figured in the increased exposure of children to sex.

Our values and our roles have changed, and we have become a more permissive society. Birth control methods have improved. Parental authority has decreased, and peers have taken on a more important role in the child's development. A generation has grown up with the constant threat of nuclear disaster, leading in some cases to a fatalistic, "Let's live it up while we can," attitude. All these factors have contributed to earlier exposure of modern youth to sex.

Single-Parent Families. There has also been an increase in divorce and in single-parent families. This can create less supervision because the single parent will most likely have to work. It can also lead to greater exposure to sexual behavior. Children in a single-parent family may witness the courting of parents by one or more suitors and more overt displays of affection. There may even be overnight "guests" in some instances.

There are other pressures that divorce and single-parent families may put on younger people. Arguments, silent meals, and general bad feelings will certainly have an effect on children. They also may find themselves in the middle of a tug-of-war for their affections, with each parent seeking to have the children see them as "in the right." Custody battles and the separation from one parent inevitably take their toll on the children.

Once a household becomes a single-parent family for whatever reason (divorce, separation, or death of a parent), children invariably have stressful adjustments to make. They may have increased responsibilities and chores, and one child may even be made responsible for a large part of the rearing of a younger sibling. Children may also have increased responsibility for making or helping to make decisions.

When a single parent works, there is a separation that the child must deal with every day. This can be particularly difficult after the child has just dealt with the separation from the other parent. The child may also have to deal with and get used to car pools, baby sitters, camp, and so on, and may have to get used to being in new situations. This may be very difficult for children with certain personalities.

Other Problems at Home

Two-career families can also create many of the same kinds of problems. The child is forced to deal with more independence, responsibilities, and contact with others and new situations.

A problem home situation can also be stressful for children with both parents. Aside from the decaying marriage, there can be a particularly strict or lenient home situation. Parents may also be under stress and take it out on everyone at home. Even when not actively using family members as scapegoats, there will be obvious stress in the parent that the child will notice and to which he or she will react. A crowded home situation, with its lack of privacy and unavoidable conflicts, can create stress. Money problems can be stressful to both parents and children; one or more family members may be involved with alcohol or drugs. Even in the best of homes children will pick up on things from adults, such as their little fears and idiosyncrasies. This will create stress in the child, which can be worsened by the child not yet being able to perceive the situation correctly and thus magnifying the problem. A child cannot analyze situations the way adults can and may not have the proper background and information to do so. Little fears in the adult may then turn into great fears in the child.

Stress at School

School can also be a major source of pressure and stress for young people. Again, there is the pressure for success, which can come from parents and teachers. Stress may also result from labeling. A child labeled as "bright" or as "underachieving" has great pressure to perform well. A child labeled as "slow" or as a "troublemaker" has other types of pressure put on him. The child who is expected to fail has the added stress of being in a frustrating situation without any support or encouragement. The failure will most likely continue (become a self-fulfilling prophecy), as will the stress that accompanies it.

Large classes in schools have inherent problems. Time may be wasted on the mechanics of classes changing, having homework checked, and so on. This leads to all kinds of possibly stressful situations as kids become bored sitting and writing. There is extra temptation to talk, and fool around while the same pressure is there to absorb a great deal of information and to do well. In any classroom, discipline problems occur, but especially in a crowded classroom. Small classrooms and large class sizes make conditions more conducive to problems, particularly in interactions between children. It is also not a good atmosphere for many enjoyable activities because there just may not be room. Of course, individual attention is minimal, and busy-work may be extensively assigned. In any class situation, teachers may have their "pet" students, which can have a poor effect on the other students. The average quiet child, who does not cause any trouble and does not attract attention by performing either superior or poor work, may be ignored as attention is given to the exceptional, failing, or troublesome students.

Another stressor in school may be the speed with which tasks must be accomplished. Students rush from class to class and subject to subject. It is necessary to work quickly to keep up with the pace. Allowances may not be made for the slower worker, who is nevertheless very competent. Homework has to be done, reports become due, and tests must be given preparation time; deadlines are a fact of school life.

Still another potential stressor in school is boredom. For the quick child, waiting may be a major part of the day. Children spend six to seven hours a day in school and may not be given much freedom of movement or even the freedom to use the bathroom as necessary. School subjects, too, can seem meaningless to the child. School burnout can thus become a very serious problem.

In some schools children are faced with the threat of violence. Even in the best areas there can be problems with bullies or children ganging up on one child. Interpersonal conflicts between children or between a student and a teacher can be a source of stress, as can a tough teacher. There can be personality clashes even between "nice" kids or with "good" teachers. Trying to gain peer approval can lead to worry about being popular, getting invited to parties, and dating. All of these factors are very real sources of stress in young people.

Children can also be cruel to one another. An unusual name, a handicap (even as slight as a minor speech impediment), wearing glasses, being smarter than or not as smart as one's peers, not being good looking, dressing poorly, being poor, or being different in any way can lead to teasing, shame, and stress.

Some other stressful school-related situations for children are tryouts for an athletic team, cheerleading, a singing group, or a band, and rushing to get to school on time. Speaking in front of a group can be an extremely stressful experience for many children. This situation may occur frequently, as students often are called on to answer in class. The act of merely sitting in a classroom may be stressful, particularly when it must be done for hours on end and in one position.

The nature of school systems or individuals in them can add to the problems children face. There is pressure on administrators to produce a better product. As a result, there may be an emphasis on the teaching of skills and facts while content and comprehension are sacrificed. Teaching for tests may be the main aim, especially in school systems where teaching effectiveness is measured by test scores.

Although children may look and act like adults, they are not adults and may not be ready for some of the adult situations in which they find themselves. Growing up is difficult, and can be even harder when rushed.

Realize, of course, that amid all of these disheartening scenarios, most children cope fairly well and that even in great adversity, some seem invulnerable to the effects of stress.

LESSON 2

Purpose: To show the children that their experiences are not unique; that other children experience the same things.

Materials Needed

Tape I, Side 1, Dialogue 1
Workbook Activities 2-1, 2-2, 2-3, 2-4, and 2-5

Directions

1. Begin by talking about the things that make you feel good, the things you like to do, and the places you like to visit. Write these on the chalkboard. Then write a list of things that get you upset, frightened, or angry. Think of examples from the school situation as well so that the children can identify with them.

2. Erase the lists on the chalkboard and do the same thing for the class as a whole. Make a list of things that they like and a list of things that upset them. Include all answers. Remember that not everyone experiences the same things in the same way.

3. Have the students make their own list in their workbooks on Activity 2-1. They should include only those items on the class list that apply to them and any other personal ones.

4. Explain that the tape is going to talk about some other children and the kinds of things they experience.

5. Play Tape I, Side 1, Dialogue 1. (The dialogue follows this lesson.)

6. When the tape is finished, ask the children to add anything else to their lists that they have thought of after listening to the tape.

Follow-up Suggestions

1. Using Activity 2-2, have the children keep a log of the stressors they encounter over a period of several days.

2. Have the children use Activity 2-3 to check off the stresses that apply to them. The students may add the newly recognized ones to their earlier lists.

3. Have the children write a story entitled "What a Day," Activity 2-4. This can be about a good or bad day, either factual or fictional. Encourage students to describe what happened, how the events happened, how they felt, and how they reacted to them.

4. Have the children mark off and total those stresses they have experienced over the past year using the Holmes–Rahe Life Stress Inventory in Activity 2-5. A score of over 150 may indicate that the student is likely to experience problems due to stress; a score of over 300 indicates an even greater risk. These children should realize that they have had a particularly high stress load this year and should be more aware that they may need to be concerned about relaxation.

TAPE I, SIDE 1, DIALOGUE 1

Life can be hard when you're growing up. Grownups think that kids have it easy. They say that all we have to do is go to school and play and that they take care of us so we really have nothing to worry about. Well, grownups aren't so smart after all. They don't know everything. Kids have plenty of things to worry about. Here are some stories that illustrate some of the problems that children may encounter. I'll bet you find that a few of them are not very different from some of the problems that you come up against.

Hi. I guess I'll go first. I might as well get it over with. I get nervous when I have to speak in front of people, so the longer I wait around for my turn, the more nervous I'll get. And boy, can I get nervous! I start to sweat all over. Sometimes it even shows up on my clothes. Then I get even more nervous and embarrassed. My hands get kind of wet and clammy too, and I don't want to shake anyone's hand or touch them because I'm afraid they'll notice. My mouth gets real dry too. It's sort of like when the dentist puts that little plastic thing in my mouth and it sucks up the saliva. You know the one I mean? I start breathing really fast and hard also and I can feel my heart going faster. I'll tell you, I sure don't like it, but I just can't help it. Anyway, I'll get this over quickly so that I can calm down and get back to normal. My name is Herman Angel Arnspengel. Now don't laugh. That's my name. My parents gave it to me. I didn't ask for it. It just came with the territory. And that's what I'm going to talk about. You see, my name is my problem. I hate it. Everyone teases me about it. It makes me so angry that it feels like my blood is boiling. I get red in the face and usually I start yelling. The muscles in my neck get all tight too. I can't help it. It just happens. But that all makes things even worse. Everybody makes fun of me just so that they can see me get angry. They're so mean. They think it's a free show. I can hear them now. "Well, could it be that Herman Angel Arnspengel is getting angry? Yes, he is. Uh, uh Herman. You mustn't get angry." Oooh. I could kill them when they do that. I just make a fist and tighten up my arms and my arms start shaking. But I can't just hit them every time they do it. I'd be in a fight ten times a day, every day, so I just stand there and steam.

It's not just me that gets made fun of, though. Kids can be really mean. Sal D'Azano has a lisp. That's not his fault, of course, but they tease him about it all the time. "Tho Thal, what'th cookin'? It'th a nith day, ithn't it?," they'd say. He'd just smile, but I can tell that it really hurts him inside.

Then there's Billy Blake. He's real smart and he wears glasses and the kids are just jealous of him. They call him Billy the four-eyed braniac. Sometimes they won't even let him play in the games. Sometimes I think that one of the reasons he's so smart is that since everybody freezes him out of things he has nothing better to do than study anyway.

Sally Anderson gets it too. She has a big nose and she's not very pretty. But she's really a nice girl. She takes it worse than any of them. The kids make fun of her nose and call her Pinocchio. She starts to cry. I feel sorry for her. Sometimes she just breaks down and sobs. Her whole body shakes and she can't catch her breath. They leave her alone when she gets that upset, but they just start again a few days later.

Just to mention two more, the other kids pick on Alfie Riggs because he's fat and because he isn't very good at sports. They run away after they tease him, though. He's not just fat. He's strong too. He'll hit anybody that he hears making fun. He can't run very fast to catch anyone, but when he does, watch out! He gets crazy. He screams and curses and his head shakes a lot. It's not right of him to be like that, but it can really get to you when people make fun. Take it from me. And the other thing that doesn't seem fair is

Tape I, Side 1, Dialogue 1, continued

that Alfie is always the one who gets in trouble. It never seems to be the ones who make fun of him.

I may even feel the worst for Janet Davis. She's a really quiet, sweet girl. She hardly ever says anything at all. Her problem is that she's very poor. Everyone knows it too. Even if you didn't know it, you could tell right away. All you have to do is to look at the clothes that she wears. They're old and out of style. They're torn and don't even fit very well. Probably they're hand-me-downs. She tries, though. They're always clean and all, but they never look very good. And she always stays home when we go on trips. She says she doesn't want to go, but everyone knows that she can't afford it. Our teacher, Mrs. Green, offered to pay for her once. Charlie Young overheard her ask. Janet said she wouldn't take any money that she couldn't pay back. She's really a good person, but the kids still make fun of her and call her "Rags Davis." I think that's why she's always so quiet. She gets real embarrassed. She holds her hands together in front of her or just rocks from one foot to the other. She looks so uncomfortable. And she turns red and just sort of shrinks down. She really looks smaller because she doesn't stand up straight. I get the feeling that she'd like to shrink down and disappear. She doesn't yell or anything, but I can see her face kind of tighten up and she closes her mouth tight. I can see her forehead wrinkle up and it looks like she's even grinding her teeth together. She won't show her anger, but she's angry.

I guess I don't have it as bad as some of the people I just told you about, but that doesn't make it any better when the kids are picking on me. It hurts.

Hi. I'm Lisa Dixon and I'm up next for all you listeners out there in cassette land. Nobody makes fun of me, that's not my problem. As a matter of fact, getting along with other kids has never been my problem. Last year I was voted most popular in the class and this year I'm president of the class. I've got a different kind of problem. It's school and schoolwork that does me in. I try hard, but I guess I'm just not that brilliant. I never can seem to understand things as well as it seems I should. I could put three hours of studying in for a test and still sweat it out whether I fail with a 60 or just pass with a 65. I get so jealous of kids like Billy Blake. He gets great marks. Then there's Jimmy Hughes who gets good marks without even putting any work into it. Why can't I be like that? Oh, what I'd give for their brains and their memory. Everybody thinks I'm so cool and calm and in control, but I'm not like that at all when it comes to school work. Whenever there's a test coming up I don't sleep well at night. I toss and turn and worry. I can't stop thinking about the test no matter how hard I try. It's like someone else has control of my mind. All I can think of is that test. I try to think of my boyfriend or a song I like, but my thoughts go back to the test. I try not to think of anything and the test still pops into my head. It just drives me crazy and then I'm tired the next day because I didn't sleep enough. Of course, I can't concentrate that well on the test when I'm tired. I can't win.

That's not all. During class I'm always thinking that Mrs. Green may call on me for an answer. I feel nervous all day long about that. And then when she does call on me— oh boy! Whether I know the answer or not I get this funny feeling up and down my back. It's like an electric shock. I guess it's fear because it's the same feeling that I get at a scary movie when all of a sudden the killer jumps out. My arms get real tight. My legs do too. I feel myself bite down hard with my jaw and sometimes I even shake a little. I can't control it. Some cool, calm girl, huh? I wonder if any of the other kids notice it. I worry about whether they do, and that makes it worse. Not only do I get scared, but I get embarrassed too. I know I get all red and I can even feel myself sweat. Everybody says

Tape I, Side 1, Dialogue 1, continued

that I make a funny face too, but I don't even notice myself doing it. It's a good thing that I am popular and I have friends so that I can enjoy the other things in school. If it was all as bad as the tests and the questions, I'd go nuts.

I'm Craig. I really don't have a school problem, although it could happen in school too. My stress gets to me on my way home from school and around my neighborhood. There's this big kid named Jake who hangs out around my block. He doesn't even live there but he's always hanging out in front of my building or the one next door. Sometimes he's alone and sometimes he's with other big kids. I guess they're sort of a gang. Well, my problem is this. Every time I pass by (and I have to pass by to get to my house) they do something. Some days they take my money. Sometimes they hit me or push me in the bushes. Sometimes they throw my books in the street and sometimes they just yell and pretend that they're going to do something just so that they can scare me and make fun of me. All the way home from school I'm thinking about how I've got to pass by them. I get a picture in my mind of Jake hitting me and I make a face and wince and I sweat and get tight and start breathing hard. It's like Lisa gets when she's getting a test only it's worse because I know that I'll probably be getting beaten up very soon. Sometimes I can't stop myself from shaking. Not only do I get scared and get that same crazy feeling up and down my spine, but I get angry too. It's not fair that I have to put up with this. I just want to hit Jake so badly that I feel like I'll burst. I know that it's not like in the movies, though. He's really a big kid and he's much older and bigger than me and he's got his whole gang. I'd really get hurt badly if I ever did hit him back. But I'll tell you, it could drive you crazy to have to put up with it.

My name is Edith and I have a problem too. I do things slowly. I like to work slowly and my work is much better when I work slowly. But it seems like I'm at one speed and the rest of the world is at another speed. It's sort of like I'm on the 33⅓ setting on a record player, kind of like when it plays real slow…and everybody else is at 78 r.p.m.'s like this…It starts at home. I'm the last to finish eating and someone else is already cleaning up around me and yelling at me to hurry. It makes me eat too fast and I feel all gassy. My stomach is upset a lot because of everybody always yelling at me to hurry. It happens when we're going somewhere also. I'm still getting dressed and everybody else is ready and yelling at me. I'll admit that sometimes I really am late, but sometimes I'm not and it's just that everybody is just so rushed and impatient. At school the same thing happens. I'm doing my work as well and as carefully as I can and the teacher says that we should all be done by now and that we have to put things away. It seems like I never get to finish anything. Homework takes me twice as long as it takes my friends. It seems like my whole life is spent trying to do things in time for deadlines that somebody has given me. I can never finish a test on time, so I always lose points on questions that I knew the answers to. It's just that I didn't get up to them. I see everybody rushing all around in this world and it just doesn't look healthy. I really think I should be allowed to do things slowly, but the world doesn't seem to let me.

I'm Ricky. I just went through a really rough experience. It's called tryouts. In my case, I tried out for the school baseball team. It's the same with all tryouts, though. I spoke to some of the other kids at school who tried out for the chorus, the band, and for parts in the school play, and they said the same thing about everything. The kids who ran for office at school like Betsy Wong and Warren Jamison, who both ran for class president, said that they went through the same kinds of things too. Even my older brother, Fred, said that he had the same feelings when he tried to get into different high

Tape I, Side 1, Dialogue 1, continued

schools. He had to take tests and personal interviews and everything. What happened to all of us was that we were so nervous along the way that we really didn't perform as well as we could have. I made two errors on easy ground balls hit to me and my friend Alan missed a swing at a pitch so badly that the bat flew out of his hand. The tension had made our muscles so tight and had made our minds wander so that we couldn't concentrate well. The worst part was when the results of the tryouts were read. Both of us just stood there sweating, with dry mouths and hearts that were beating so fast and loudly that they sounded like drums. Alan made the team and I didn't. I'm all right now, but I took it pretty badly at first. I was disappointed and then I thought of the shame when everybody would ask me how I did and I'd have to tell them that I had failed. I almost cried, but I couldn't let anybody see me do that. It's hard to risk failing, and it's even harder when you really do fail at something.

I'm Sally and I've really got problems. I live with my mother, my father (actually, he's my stepfather), my grandparents, and six brothers and sisters. Things here at school are fine, but once I leave, my life is miserable. My mom and my father got divorced. I took that really hard. As if that wasn't enough, my stepfather and I don't get along at all. I get yelled at a lot and I've had a few real beatings too. As soon as my stepfather starts on one of his crazy yelling fits I can feel my jaw get tight and my teeth start to grind against each other. My eyes close a little and my forehead wrinkles up a lot. It's as if I'm expecting to get hit and I'm protecting myself. Sometimes he gets drunk and then he's really impossible to be with. I just cut out when he gets like that. That's when I usually get in trouble. Somehow, whenever I hang out on the streets something happens. Even when he's not crazy, things at home are tough. With all those people, it gets kind of crowded. There really isn't anywhere that I can feel is my own space, and I get no privacy. I get so jealous of other kids in the class whose home life sounds like it is so calm and quiet and trouble free.

These children have problems, that's for sure. Were any of them the same kinds that you have? Think about some other stresses that you come across so that you can discuss them with your class. And now, everyone have a real nice day—and I hope you enjoy this cassette program.

Things That Make Me Feel Good and Things That Upset Me

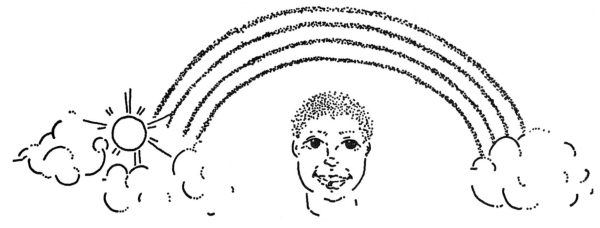

Things That Make Me Feel Good

_____

_____

_____

_____

_____

Things That Upset Me

_____

_____

_____

_____

Name _____

Date _____

Stress in My Day

DIRECTIONS: Keep a log of the stressors you encounter over a period of four days.

	Day 1	Day 2	Day 3	Day 4
Before School				
In School				
After School, Through Dinner				
After Dinner				

Stress Checklist

DIRECTIONS: On the checklist below, put a checkmark on the line before those things that make you feel stress.

_____ Fear of dying
_____ Worry about the world situation and possible war
_____ Fear of getting hurt by others
_____ Too much responsibility
_____ Too little responsibility
_____ Fear of inadequacy and failing
_____ New school
_____ New neighborhood
_____ New class
_____ New crowd I hang around with
_____ Jealous of brothers or sisters
_____ Not feeling as if I'm accomplishing anything (no real purpose)
_____ Not enough power to get things that I want done
_____ No privacy at home
_____ Crowded home
_____ Conditions at home are physically not good (too dirty, messy, poor)
_____ Not enough heat or too hot at home
_____ Not enough food
_____ Sick or handicapped person at home to care for
_____ Someone at home on drugs or too much alcohol
_____ Parents separated or divorced
_____ One or both parents dead
_____ Living with other relative or friend (but parents alive)
_____ Parent has boyfriends or girlfriends around that I don't like
_____ Person physically picks on me (at home or in the neighborhood)
_____ I'm picked on because of wearing glasses, my name, physical appearance, my dress, a handicap or impediment, or other
_____ I am handicapped
_____ I always rush to get reports or homework done on time
_____ I never have enough time to study enough for tests
_____ Decisions are hard for me
_____ I don't get along with certain teachers
_____ I don't get along with some students
_____ School bores me
_____ I can't speak in class or in front of a group
_____ Teachers or students think I am "bad" or "stupid" and they act according to that label and not to how I really am

_____ I have too many chores or responsibilities at home
_____ I am responsible for too many decisions at home
_____ I am not maturing physically at the speed I would like
_____ I don't like my neighborhood
_____ I don't have enough money
_____ I worry about getting beaten up by certain people
_____ I don't have enough friends
_____ I am impatient and can't wait when I have to
_____ I am not popular
_____ I get nervous with members of the opposite sex
_____ I get nervous when I try out for things (clubs, teams, etc.)
_____ Someone I know well has been put in jail or an institution
_____ I am not healthy
_____ I was fired from a job
_____ I want to work but can't find a job
_____ I just broke up with my boyfriend or girlfriend
_____ Someone in my family just had a big change in their health
_____ There is a new child in my family
_____ A friend or family member recently died
_____ A friend recently moved away
_____ I have just or am about to leave home
_____ I have just received a great award or honor
_____ School is ending soon for me
_____ I am much more or less active at church lately
_____ I spend much more or less time at recreation lately
_____ I get embarrassed easily
_____ I don't fit in
_____ I don't like the way I look
_____ I have a drinking or drug problem
_____ Friends put pressure on me to do things I don't want to do
_____ I have a new step-parent
_____ OTHER STRESS (Write these below):

What a Day!

DIRECTIONS: On the lines below, write about a good or bad day you have had. You can even write a fictional story if you prefer. Describe what happened, how things happened, how you felt, and how you reacted.

_____

_____

_____

_____

_____

_____

_____

_____

_____

_____

_____

_____

_____

_____

_____

_____

_____

_____

_____

_____

_____

_____

_____

Stress Inventory

DIRECTIONS: Circle the number (mean value) next to each life event that has happened to you in the last year. When you've gone through the entire list, add up your score. The higher the total score, the more stress you've experienced.

The Holmes–Rahe Life Stress Inventory
The Social Readjustment Rating Scale
(modified for children)

Life Event	Mean Value
1. A parent has died	100
2. Parents have divorced	73
3. Parents have separated	65
4. Separation from parents (at boarding school or living with another family)	63
5. Death of a close family member	63
6. Major personal injury or illness	53
7. Remarriage of a parent (getting a new parent)	50
8. A parent was fired from a job *or* you were expelled from school	47
9. Parents got back together after separating	45
10. One parent stops working to stay at home *or* parent goes back to work	45
11. Major change in health or behavior of family member	44
12. Pregnancy of a family member	40
13. Problems in school	39
14. Gaining a new family member (e.g., birth, adoption, grandparent moves in)	39
15. Major school change (e.g., class or teacher change, failing subjects)	39
16. Family financial state changes a great deal (much better or worse off)	38
17. Death or serious illness of a close friend	37
18. A new activity begins (one that takes up a lot of time and energy, e.g., dance or music lessons, sports team, computer classes after school)	36
19. Major change in the number of arguments with parents or brothers and sisters	35
20. Feeling threatened (trouble with a bully or a gang)	31
21. Losing or being robbed of a valuable or important possession	30
22. Major change in responsibilities at home (e.g., must help with many chores or with raising a younger child)	29
23. Brother or sister leaves home (e.g., runs away, joins army, goes away to school)	29
24. Trouble with relatives other than parents or siblings (e.g., grandparents, aunt, uncle)	29
25. Outstanding personal achievement and recognition	28
26. Major change in living conditions (e.g., neighborhood gets much improved, fire damages part of home)	25
27. Personal habits change (e.g., style of dress, manners, people you hang out with)	24

The Holmes–Rahe Life Stress Inventory
The Social Readjustment Rating Scale
(modified for children)

Life Event	Mean Value
28. Trouble with a teacher	23
29. Major change in your school schedule or conditions (e.g., new school schedule, more work demanded, using a temporary building)........	20
30. Change in where you live (even in the same building)	20
31. Changing to a new school....................................	20
32. Major change in usual type or amount of recreation (e.g., more or less time to play).......................................	19
33. Major change in religious activities..............................	19
34. Major change in school activities (e.g., clubs, movies, visiting friends)...	18
35. Major change in sleep habits...................................	16
36. Major change in family get-togethers (many more or less)...........	15
37. Major change in eating habits..................................	15
38. Vacation..	13
39. Christmas or birthday.......................................	12
40. Punished for doing wrong.....................................	11
Total	

Source: Adapted and reprinted with permission from *Journal of Psychosomatic Research,* Vol. II, Thomas Holmes and Richard Rahe, "Holmes–Rahe Social Readjustment Rating Scale," 1967, Pergamon Press, Ltd.

LESSON 3

Breathing

BACKGROUND FOR THE TEACHER

The relationship between good health and breathing has been recognized for a long time. Centuries ago, people in India, China, and Japan emphasized breath control. They realized that if you improve the quality of your breathing, you can increase your feeling of well-being.

Breathing supplies the body with the energy we need to maintain life. The act of breathing, or the exchange of gases, is called respiration. Respiration involves breathing in (inhalation or inspiration), breathing out (exhalation or expiration), and a brief pause after exhalation. This process involves pulling oxygen from the air into the lungs, mixing it with blood (which carries the gas to the tissues), and carrying off the carbon dioxide (which is eliminated by the cells, as a waste product). It is initiated by a signal from the brain.

Air comes in and out of the body through the respiratory tract, which includes the nose, pharynx, trachea, the two branches of the bronchi, and the alveoli. The air comes through the nose, where it is prepared for the lungs by being warmed, moistened, and filtered. It travels down through the trachea and bronchi and ends in the tiny alveolar sacs. It is in the alveoli that gases (oxygen and carbon dioxide) are exchanged and get into the blood. The lungs themselves do not move. The action of respiration is mainly carried out by the diaphragm, a large dome-shaped muscular sheet that attaches to the base of the rib cage and top of the abdomen. As you breathe in, the ribs and diaphragm expand outward and upward. As you breathe out, they close downward.

This procedure is basically controlled by the autonomic (involuntary) nervous system. However, since muscles, tendons and joints are involved, breathing comes under voluntary control and can be interfered with. The quality of our breathing (through both the voluntary and involuntary nervous systems) is affected by the pressures of daily living. When you are tense or upset, your breathing becomes shallow and irregular, your heart rate increases, and the muscles in your abdomen tighten, making good breathing even more difficult. You can, however, become aware of when you hold your breath and, by slowing and deepening your breathing, you can help trigger relaxation.

You can also begin to change your awareness of how you breathe and can speed the recovery of your breath to normal after a momentary pause. You are breathing ideally when you can react to a situation with an appropriate response and quickly return to normal functioning. By being aware of your breathing and by practicing breathing exercises, you can improve the quality and functioning of your breath.

LESSON 3

Purpose: To help the children improve the awareness, quality, and functioning of their breathing.

Materials Needed

Tape I, Side 1, Dialogue 2
Workbook Activity 3-1

Directions

1. Tell the children that proper breathing is the first—and easiest—way for a person to calm down. Ask the students to tense themselves for ten seconds and to imagine themselves very upset, then ask them if they held their breath. Most students will say they did. Explain that when people are upset they usually change their breathing pattern. Let the students know that they are going to learn a way of breathing that will help them become calm any time they are upset. This technique can be used 50 times a day or more, if necessary, because it only takes a short time to do.

2. Ask the children to blow on their hands to notice that their breath is warm. Then ask these questions:

- What does your breathing feel like right now?
- Do you breathe in through your nose or your mouth?
- Can you see any movement in your body when you breathe normally?
- Is there a gentle rise in your chest? In your abdomen?
- Is there more movement in your chest or abdomen?

Now have the students place a hand on their chests while they breathe in and out. Ask them to notice how it feels. Then have the children put a hand on their ribs, and finally on their bellies. Where do they feel the most movement?

Try this experiment. Have students breathe in and out using just the upper part of their chests. Then have the students breathe in and out using only the rib cage and chest. Does this feel different? Now have them start the breath low in the belly, breathing through the nose. Explain that the diaphragm will move downward and air will fill the middle of the torso and then the whole upper chest. This is the ideal way to breathe in. The students then let the air out through the nose or mouth, and the chest and ribs sink. Ask the students to let all the air out of their lungs without forcing it. Excess effort during inhalation or exhalation is not necessary. Remind the children that all movements should be gentle.

3. Ask the children to turn to Activity 3-1 in their workbooks. Use the material as a reading lesson that may be read together orally or silently, or that you may read aloud. Supplement this with any of the other information from the "Background for the Teacher" section you feel is appropriate.

4. Play Tape I, Side 1, Dialogue 2. (The dialogue follows this lesson.)

5. Point out that the tape's "skinny breathing" exercise is just that, an exercise. The correct way to breathe is to have the stomach and chest expand when inhaling.

Follow-up Suggestions

1. Throughout the day, every day, have the children notice their breathing. Ask them to try to take a few long, deep breaths while waiting for the school bus, during a television commercial, or before a school lesson.

Have the children try to notice their breathing to see whether there are times when they hold their breath, when it is irregular or shallow, and when it is the deepest. Have the students pay particular attention to their breathing pattern during and after a strenuous activity.

2. Set up times in your daily schedule to do deep breathing. Check to see if the children have been able to schedule times during the day to take long, full breaths. Could they detect any differences in their breathing before and after listening to the breathing tape?

3. Here is an easy exercise your students can do to increase their breathing capacity: Breathe in slowly to a count of four and hold the breath for four counts. Then, at the same slow speed, let the air out for at least six counts. This can gradually be increased over a period of time to "in" for eight counts, "hold" for four, and "out" for ten.

Caution the children against changing too much, too soon. If they try to increase their breathing capacity too much right away, they may get dizzy. They should find what count feels normal and comfortable, and should only move up one extra count every day or even every few days. Soon they will have increased their capacity.

Remind children to breathe deeply all the time and to try their deep, slow breathing in stressful situations. The breathing alone, without any other relaxation skills, may help relax some children a great deal, so try to make time to allow them to practice.

TAPE I, SIDE 1, DIALOGUE 2

I'd like you to get into a comfortable position where you are supported and your torso, from your waist up, is as straight as possible, without straining. We are going to work on our breathing. First of all, I'd like you to notice how your breathing feels right now. Close your eyes. Without changing it, can you notice the speed of your breathing? Can you feel where the breath seems to start? Is it in your belly? Up in your chest? Just take a moment to notice what the act of breathing feels like, from the inhalation through your nose to the exhalation.

Now I'd like you to try to slow down both the inhalation and the exhalation. Take as long as you can to breathe in and out. You might imagine that your torso is a container that you are slowly filling with liquid, starting low in the belly and rising to the chest clear up to the neck. Let it out the same way and empty the container. Try this a few times now,

Tape I, Side 1, Dialogue 2, continued

nice and slow. Good. Now breathe normally. The next time you take a long breath I want you to hold it for as long as possible before you let it out. Do that now. Now breathe normally. I'd like you to hold your breath again, but this time when you let the air out, I want you to make a loud hissing noise. You will sound like an old tire or a loud snake. This will get rid of a lot of old air in your lungs. Try not to take a quick, big breath, but be gentle. You should not use much shoulder or chest movement to inhale. Try it now. Let's hear that hiss. Try that again. Rest a moment and then take another breath and hiss on the exhalation.

Open your eyes now and just breathe normally for a while. We are going to be doing what we call fat and skinny breathing. You will be blowing up your abdomen like a balloon, making it very fat, and then letting it get very skinny like the air is going out of the balloon. I'd like you to first put your hand on your belly. Put your thumb on your belly button and spread your fingers. Now try to be sure that your hand moves out as you blow up your belly. Make your belly as fat as you can. Some of you may need to unbuckle your belt or loosen your pants if you keep them very tight. Try it now. Breathe in and make your belly fat. Did you make it rise? Try it again, hold it a moment before you let it go. Go ahead now. Good. The more you do it, the easier it will get. Now let's do the opposite. Let's make your tummy as skinny as it can be. As you breathe, pull your belly in towards the back of your chair. Hold it. When you let the air out, pull the belly in even more. Then let it go. Let's try that now. Very good. Try it again. In. Pull belly in. Hold and out. Now I'd like you to alternate between fat and skinny breathing at your own speed. Breathe normally a few times after fat and skinny breathing. It's important to breathe normally between relaxation breathing. Okay, take your hand away and breathe normally now.

This time I want you to fill up your chest like a balloon. Only fill the upper part of your body as you breathe in. How does that feel? Now would you alternate between fat tummy breathing and this chest breathing. Try it. One more time with each. Good. Open your eyes and breathe normally until we begin again.

We're going to get fancy now. You will inhale and blow up your belly, then hold it. Still holding, you will push the air up into your chest. Still holding your breath, push it back down to your belly. Keep going back and forth with a rocking motion for as long as you can. Okay. Let's close our eyes and try it. Take a breath and hold it. Push the air up to your chest. Now back down to the belly and back up. A little longer. Keep going as long as possible. When you've done it once, take a few normal breaths and try it again. Again, take a breath.

Very good. That's hard. How does your breathing feel now? Has it changed in any way? Take a moment to notice the depth and speed of your breathing. Are you breathing deeply? Try to remember during the day to notice your breathing and then to take some nice long breaths in and out. Breathe slowly and deeply. Do that a few times during the day. Feel relaxed and have a great day.

Respiration (Breathing)

DIRECTIONS: Read along with your teacher as this information on respiration is read.

Respiration

You breathe in so that you can take in oxygen, which your body absorbs into the blood and uses as fuel. You breathe out so that you can get rid of waste gases (especially carbon dioxide).

The parts of the respiratory system that do all of this are shown here:

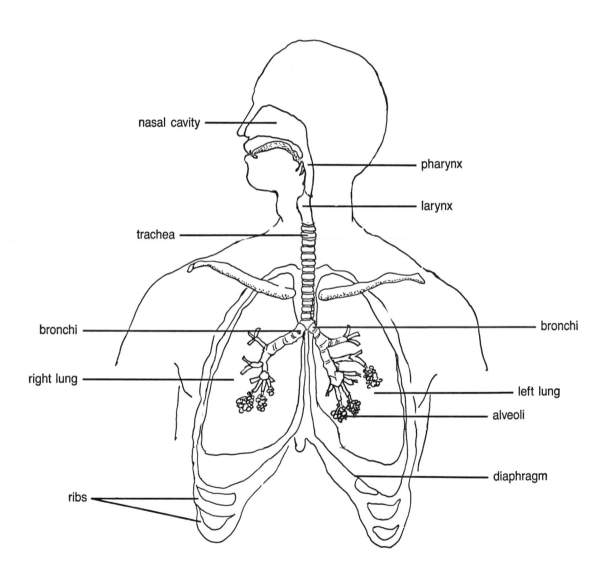

They are the nasal cavity, pharynx, larynx, trachea, bronchi, lungs, alveoli, and diaphragm. The air comes in through the nose or mouth. It is best to breathe in through the nose, because the nose warms, moistens, and cleans the air. As the air comes in it goes to the pharynx and trachea and then divides to the two bronchi and to the right and left lung. The bronchi, as you see in the diagram, divide into many tubes, which also divide and finally end in little sacs (bags) called alveoli. This is where the exchange of air takes place. Only some of the air that we inhale reaches these alveoli and is used in respiration. A large part of it just stays in the tubes and is exhaled. We need to exhale this extra air because it takes up space that we need for new, fresh air, and because it contains waste products sent out by the cells and muscles. This is why it is important to breathe in deeply to get as much new oxygen in *and* to breathe out deeply to get rid of as much waste air as we can and to make room for new, fresh air.

The lungs themselves have no muscle power. The muscles around the rib cage, and of the diaphragm itself, are used for breathing. As we breathe in and out, the muscles expand and collapse the rib cage. The diaphragm is very important in breathing. Although we are not positive exactly how it works, we know that the diaphragm contracts as we breathe in and it relaxes as we breathe out.

Your breathing changes depending on the amount of exercise you get, the condition of your lungs, and whether you are relaxed or under stress. You can also change your breathing pattern by practicing deep-breathing exercises like those on the taped lesson.

LESSON 4

Muscle Relaxation

BACKGROUND FOR THE TEACHER

This lesson includes a brief review of the skeletal and muscle systems and of posture. It is meant to reacquaint you, the teacher, with the information that you probably have learned, but may have forgotten over the years. The same material has been included in the students' workbooks so that all of you can discuss the information. It is helpful for the children to understand basic anatomy so that they can have an accurate picture of their bodies as they learn to control them. As with all of the lessons in this program, you have the option of using as much of the material as you feel is appropriate for your students.

LESSON 4

Purpose: To let the children learn about and experience the physiology involved in muscle relaxation.

Materials Needed

    Tape I, Side 2, Dialogue 3
    Mirror
    Workbook Activity 4-1

Directions

1. Ask the students to make a muscle. (Most of them will bend their forearm at the elbow to try to increase the size of their bicep.) Now direct them to feel the muscle with their free hand while extending the arm that is tightened. Have them do this several times, noting how the muscle feels as it contracts and releases. Have the children describe how the muscle feels as it is tightened and released.

Point out that most of the students chose to tighten the same muscle, the bicep, and that they probably made a fist at the same time, thus using many other muscles. Explain that when you said to make a muscle, they could have chosen any one of many muscles. Show them how to contract the tricep muscle by holding the arm straight out in front and making a tight fist. (See the illustrations here.)

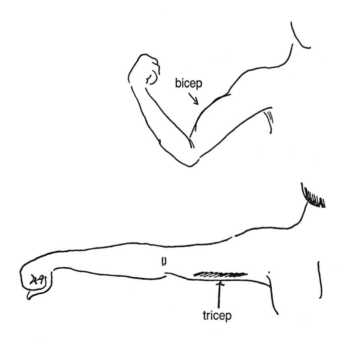

2. Ask the children to try to tighten other muscles, for example:

- The calf muscle, by tensing the leg
- The temperomandibular muscles in the side of the face, by holding the mouth closed and clenching and unclenching the teeth

Have the children clench their fists again and notice what happens to other parts of the body. How does the whole body feel when they release the fist? Point out that tightening of the fists, which people often do under stress, involves many muscles in addition to the fists. Have the students clench their fists for 30 to 60 seconds. Do they feel any discomfort from overloading the muscles?

Have the students hold a tight posture and let them study it. They should be trying to hold themselves as they would if they were upset. Try to have them notice how they are breathing and which muscles are tight (their fists, jaw, and so on). They might also use a mirror to study what this posture looks like. Using the mirror (or looking at each other), they can also compare angry expressions with relaxed, happy facial expressions.

3. A short talk on hyperactivity may be appropriate here. A hyperactive child experiences excess motor functioning, which results in overloading of the muscles. Have the students mimic a hyperactive, fast-paced, nervous child by wiggling a little and moving different parts of the body quickly. They can move their hands and heads quickly and speak rapidly. Be sure to follow this by having them try to do each action very slowly. Is one way more difficult? Is one way more pleasurable? Are both uncomfortable? You might mention that people have different body speeds. While some seem to be always like the $33\frac{1}{3}$ r.p.m. setting on the stereo, others always seem to be on 45 r.p.m., and still others on 78 r.p.m. In addition, each of us has times when our speed changes. Let students try to notice this in themselves. When they are at 78 r.p.m., it might be a good time to do relaxation exercises.

4. Mention to the students that muscles and bones work together; muscles move the bones. Have the children refer to the reading lessons on the skeletal and muscle systems and posture (in Workbook Activity 4-1). Tell them that the next tape describes step by step how to relax the muscles and that it helps to know something about the skeleton, muscles, and posture before beginning. Use your discretion as to whether to do all the material at once or to break it up into separate lessons. The lessons may be given as oral or silent reading lessons, depending on your group.

5. Discuss the following comprehension questions and answers:

- Besides supporting your weight and producing blood, what other purpose does your skeletal system serve? *(Protecting the organs.)*
- What do bones do when they ossify? *(They harden.)*
- What happens in the marrow of the bone? *(Red blood cells are produced.)*
- Which bone in your skull can move? *(The mandible, or jawbone.)*
- What do spinal disks do? *(They act as shock absorbers.)*

- Match the bone with its other name:
  1. femur   a. collarbone
  2. scapula   b. shoulder blade
  3. clavicle   c. thigh bone

  (1-c; 2-b; 3-a)

- What are the three kinds of muscle? *(Cardiac muscle, smooth muscle, and striated, or skeletal, muscle.)*

- What kind of muscle moves your bones? *(Striated, or skeletal.)*

- What are the two ways that muscles can contract? *(Isotonic contraction and isometric contraction.)*

- Pushing against a brick wall is an example of an _____ contraction. *(Isometric.)*

- When muscles are resting but still have a little tension, it is called _____. *(Tonus.)*

6. Play Tape I, Side 2, Dialogue 3. (The dialogue follows this lesson.) After the children have heard the tape several times, remind them that they may omit the tensing and simply relax.

Follow-up Suggestions

1. Have the children make charts or models of the skeletal or muscle systems. Display these around the room.

2. You might have some children do extra-credit reports on one of the problems about which they often read. For example, they might write about what causes a slipped disk, a pulled muscle, or a sprained muscle.

TAPE I, SIDE 2, DIALOGUE 3

On this tape we are going to do a special relaxation technique that concentrates on our muscles. We will be doing something similar to progressive relaxation. Progressive means "step by step," and what we're going to be doing is relaxing our body step by step, one part at a time. We're going to be tightening parts of our body up and then letting them go so that we can feel the difference between when they are tight and when they are loose. We can then just release the tightness any time that we concentrate on it by remembering what it feels like to be relaxed and then making it be that way. After you have done this tape a number of times you will not even need to do the tensing-up part. Then you will only release the tension and relax the parts of your body without first tightening them.

Sit down comfortably with your feet on the floor so that your legs aren't dangling. I want your weight supported. Put your arms on the arms of your chair or on your lap. If you have a good chair for it, rest your head on the back of the chair. I don't want you to be disturbed by anything else, so you should probably close your eyes. Take a good, deep breath and let it out. Do that again: inhale...exhale. Now relax and let your body just float away. Good. Now the first thing that I want you to do is to take your right leg and stretch it

Tape I, Side 2, Dialogue 3, continued

out a little, and lift the front of your foot off the ground a little. Do that now. Keep your heel on the ground. You should feel a little tightness in the front of your leg a few inches below the knee. It means that your muscle there is working to hold your leg in that position. Now let go and relax your leg, and feel the difference when that muscle is relaxed. Really feel it, because later on I'm going to want you to try to go back to this feeling where there is no tension in the muscles. All right, now move your leg back and keep your toes on the ground while you lift your heel. Do it now. It's almost like when a ballerina goes up on her toes. Press. You can let go and feel the difference when that muscle is relaxed. Feel the tension in the back of your leg, below the knee. Do the same with your left foot now. Lift the front of your foot. Release and notice the feeling. Lift your heel. Let it ease back down and notice how it feels when the tension is released. Next, press down with your toes, as if you are crushing a lit cigarette. Release them. Your whole foot should now feel loose and relaxed. Let your feet go. Let them just sink into the floor. All right, now we're going to forget about our feet. They should feel so relaxed that it is like they aren't even there.

I want you to now lift up your knee while your foot hangs down limp. Do it with your right foot. Your foot should feel like a shirt hanging out on a clothesline. Put your foot back down and do the same thing with your left foot. Lift…and down. When your foot is back on the ground, I want you to really concentrate on both legs and on letting go of any tension that you are holding in them. They should both feel very comfortable now. Let your feet sink into the floor and let both your legs just sink into the chair. Now concentrate on your bottom. Tighten it up and squeeze and then just let it go.

Next we're going to concentrate on the abdomen. Pull it in and make yourself skinny, and arch your back a little too. This makes it tight, and we really don't want that, so relax it now. Release any muscles that are holding it. Be sure to let your back muscles go too. Take deep breaths and observe how your abdomen and back feel. This is how they should feel, nice and relaxed.

Now bend your shoulders back, kind of like a butterfly bringing its wings back to meet behind it. Now ease them back to where they were so that your shoulders need no effort to hold them. Let them feel limp. Now lift your shoulders up so that they touch your ears. Slowly let them down until they hang loosely again. Notice how they feel now when they are relaxed. Bring your left arm straight out in front of you and move your hand back onto your stomach. Do the same thing with your right hand. Just sit like this for a few seconds and breathe deeply. Concentrate on your stomach, back, and shoulders and notice if you feel any tightness or tension in any of these places. Since you just relaxed them, you shouldn't feel much tightness, but if any area feels tight, loosen it up again. Let it go and release any tension.

Now we're going to concentrate on the arms. Lay your hands flat on the desk or on the arms of your chair, depending on where you are sitting. Lift your left hand from the elbow up to your fingers. Bring it about six inches up. Notice which muscles are working to do this. While your arm is up, drop your left wrist so that your hand hangs loosely. It should look like it is broken or like a praying mantis. Lower your whole arm back down and let it all hang as loosely as your wrist. Do this with your right arm now. Lift it up a few inches, starting at the elbow and going all the way to your hand. Let your wrist hang limply. Now lower your whole arm and let it all feel limp and soft. Now lift your left arm up from the elbow to the shoulder, but leave the front part resting still. That's it. Now slowly drop the arm and let it all just melt into the chair. Now the right arm. Lift it and then slowly let it sink in and relax. Now for the fingers. Stretch them out, both hands. First extend

Tape I, Side 2, Dialogue 3, continued

them forward as if you want to make them longer. Now stretch them sideways as far as they will go. Release them and relax them. Take five seconds and, starting at your feet, notice if anything is still tense or tight. Go up your legs. Just scan. That means to think about each part and notice if it's relaxed. Move from your feet up your legs. Keep scanning for tension. If anything feels tense, release the tension. Go from the legs to your bottom. Keep scanning and then releasing any tension. Move to your abdomen, then your chest, your shoulders, your arms and then your hands.

Let's move up to the neck now. This is an area that gets very tight with many people. First extend your head all the way up as if you are trying to make yourself taller. Reach it up. Now release it and let it slowly get to a comfortable position. Next, bend your head slightly back. You may feel a sensation in the back of your neck. These are the muscles that are working. Move your head slowly back and notice how these muscles let go of the tension. To center. Continue bending your head forward so that your chin finally touches your chest. You can feel the sensation in the side of your neck. Now slowly raise your neck back up to center. Relax. Let the muscles rest. Next, bend your head so that your right ear touches your right shoulder. Notice how you feel muscles on the right side of your neck working and notice how there is a stretching in the left side of your neck. Slowly bring your head back to center and then on down so that your left ear touches your left shoulder. Notice which muscles are working now. All right. Bring your head to center and let those muscles rest. Now turn your head so that you are looking straight out over your right shoulder. Slowly. Turn the other way so that you look over your left shoulder. Slowly. Do this all very slowly. Notice the muscles that work and especially notice how it feels when they relax. Move your head back to face front and just relax all those neck muscles. Now we're going to roll our heads. Just let your head hang down in front of you. Roll it to your left shoulder, not too fast, then behind you, to your right shoulder and back to the front. Do this two more times. Now change directions and roll it three times the other way. Do any of you feel a cracking in your neck? When you are back at center, just let your head rest comfortably so that it feels like no muscles are working to hold it up.

We're almost done relaxing our muscles, but there are a few more really important ones to get to still. These are in our face. You may not realize it, but we use muscles in our face all day long and they can get overworked. A lot of people hold tension in their face, too, and even end up with pain as a result of the overworking of facial muscles. First let's look at our jaw. This is one area that often has tension held in. Some people clench their jaw and others grind their teeth. It's a good place to concentrate on relaxation so that it can get a rest, especially for those of you that are big talkers. You know that you use your jaw muscles a lot. It is only your lower jaw that moves, by the way. As a matter of fact, it's really the only movable bone in your face. Just to see how much tension gets held there at times, clench your teeth for a few seconds. Now release it and feel the difference. Lower your jaw and open your mouth wide, as wide as you can. You will probably feel a strain. Release. Now pull the corners of your mouth open in a wide smile. Release it. Just let your jaw hang slack now. Feel how nice it feels when there is no tension in your jaw muscles. Try moving your tongue to the roof of your mouth now. Move it around the mouth. Now relax the tongue.

Let's move up to the area around our eyes. Wrinkle your forehead. Now let it go. Lift your eyebrows. Relax them. Squint, as if there is a lot of sun in your eyes. Release that area. Give a good frown, as if you are displeased about something. Feel the sensation

Tape I, Side 2, Dialogue 3, continued

between your eyebrows. Release that. Close your eyes tightly. You can feel the tension in the lids and around the eyes in front. Let the tension go and relax there. Keeping your eyes closed, look to the left. Now, without using any muscle effort, let the eyes come back to center. Do the same thing to the right now. Still keeping your eyes closed, look up. Now look to center and relax. Look down; come to center; relax.

Now let's once more scan our whole body and be sure that every part is relaxed and without any muscle tension. Start with your toes. Be sure that they are relaxed and loose. Now concentrate on your feet. Are they relaxed? Go to your legs next. Any place that feels tight or tense should be relaxed immediately. Concentrate on that. Now check your bottom again. Your whole lower part of the body should now feel loose and relaxed. Move to your abdomen now. Now to your chest. From here check your shoulders. Be sure they are hanging loosely. Check your neck. Go from there to your jaw. Let it feel loose. Next, notice your forehead and now, finally, your eyes. Just sit this way for a few seconds. It should feel good to give all of your muscles a rest. Your mind can also relax once your body does.

We are now at the end of this tape. Slowly ease yourself out of this relaxed state. Open your eyes slowly. Move your hands a little; now your feet; and then slowly get up. Have a great day.

Skeletal and Muscle Systems

DIRECTIONS: Follow along with your teacher as this information is read. Be prepared to answer the questions your teacher will ask.

You use muscles all the time; you are always tightening and releasing them. Sometimes you can use a muscle too much; and sometimes, without realizing it, you can get into the habit of holding a certain muscle tight and not letting it go. The muscles in the neck, jaw, forehead, and back are just a few examples of where this can happen. Your body can even get so used to holding a muscle tight that the tightness begins to feel normal to you and you won't even notice it. If you hold muscle tension for too long you may begin to feel pain.

The tape that you are about to hear will help you learn what it feels like when a muscle is tight, and will help you learn how to let go of the muscle tension. This will let you give your muscles a rest whenever you want and will help you relax your body.

The Skeletal System

Your skeletal system, which is made up of all your bones, has a few very important purposes: It supports and distributes your weight and acts as the framework that your body is built upon; the bones protect delicate organs from damage; and blood cells are produced inside the bones.

Since your skeletal system consists of bones, let's first talk a little about bones. Bones are much softer when you are born than they are later on. As you get older, they ossify, or harden. They also get more brittle and can break more easily. When you are fully grown, you have about 206 bones in your body. Some are tiny, like the ones inside your ear, and some are large, like your thigh bone. In the center of the bone is the living part, called the marrow; that is where your red blood cells are made.

You may hear people talk about joints. Joints are the places where the bones meet, or articulate. There are four main kinds of joints. Each kind allows for a different kind of movement. For example, the hip is a ball-and-socket joint that allows for movement in many directions. A hinge joint, like the knee, allows mostly for back and forth movement. The other two kinds of joints are pivot joints, like the wrist, and gliding joints, like those in the spine.

A liquid is secreted at the joints to lubricate them, much like oil in a car. This liquid is called synovial fluid.

Even though many bones move freely, the only one in your skull that does is the mandible, or jawbone. Put your hand on your mouth and move it. You will feel that only the lower jaw moved, *not* the upper part.

The spine is an important part of the skeletal system. It has curves so that your weight gets distributed well. This also helps you in moving. In addition, the spine has many nerves going in and out of it. There are 29 bones, called vertebrae, in the spine. Between each vertebra is a piece of connective tissue, called a disk, that acts as a shock absorber. If the spine is not lined up properly, there can be a problem with the transfer of your weight, which can cause movement problems and possibly injury. Poor posture, which can be a bad habit that you pick up over the years, can also affect the balance of the weight, resulting in pain and movement problems.

The rib cage protects your heart, lungs, and other internal organs and helps in breathing.

Some other important bones are the collarbone (clavicle), shoulder blade (scapula), upper arm (humerus), forearm (radius and ulna), and thigh (femur).

The illustrations here show the front and back views of the skeleton.

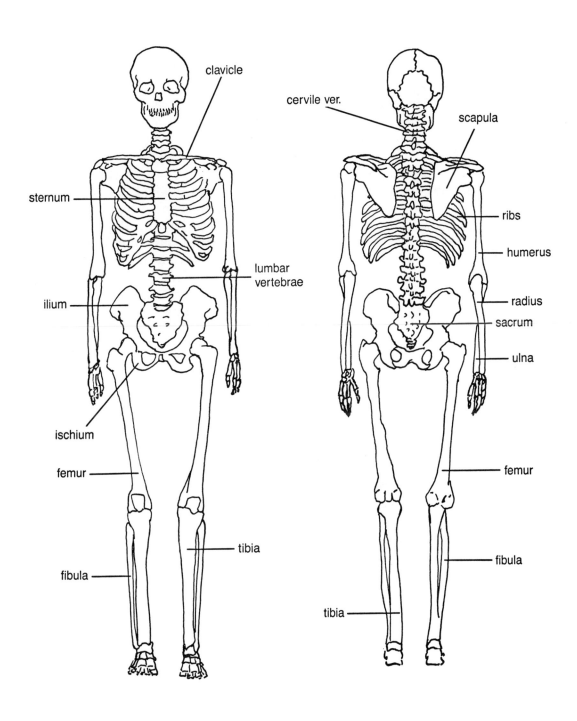

The Muscle System

There are three kinds of muscles in the body. The heart has special muscles of its own, called cardiac muscles. There are muscles inside your body, called smooth muscles, that move things through your body. An example would be the stomach muscles and the muscles in the intestines that move food along. The muscles in the glands and blood vessels are also smooth muscles. The third kind of muscle is striated muscle. These are also called skeletal muscles, since they move the bones. These are the ones with which you are probably the most familiar, and these are the ones that we are going to study.

There are more than 600 skeletal muscles in the body. They may be attached to bones, cartilage, or ligaments. Muscles are attached to bones by tendons. Bones are connected to other bones by ligaments.

When your nervous system sends signals to the muscles, they contract, and the parts of the body that are attached to them move. For example, in the breathing section, you saw that muscles move the rib cage as we breathe. When you extend your arm and pull it back up, your brain must send signals to the muscles to contract, or shorten.

Muscles can contract in two different ways. An isotonic contraction changes the length of a muscle. An isotonic contraction occurs when you hit a baseball. Isometric contractions cause hardly any change in the length of the muscle. An isometric contraction occurs when you push against the sides of the doorway.

Muscles work together in groups to produce movement. One contracts or shortens to produce the movement. This one is called the agonist, or prime mover. Another muscle has to lengthen at the same time so that the bone can move. This one is called the antagonist. When you develop muscles you should try to remember this and work on balancing out which one shortens and which one lengthens so that one doesn't get too developed while the other gets weak and flabby.

Even when you are resting, muscles have a certain amount of tension. This is called tonus. Sometimes there is too much tension, or energy is being used for no reason. There can be constant contraction. Stress, emotional strain and poor posture can cause this. Of course, the muscle can then get overworked and there can even be pain. One place that many people have too much muscle tension is in the jaw. You have to have a little tension there so the jaw doesn't just hang down, but many people clench the jaw tightly or even grind their teeth because of tension, anger, or nervousness. This can cause pain, can be uncomfortable, and can cause problems with your teeth.

The illustrations on the following page show some of the more important muscles. You can see which ones move your head and neck, your arms, legs, etc. Muscles also protect your digestive organs, move the trunk of your body, hold your spine straight, and keep your posture.

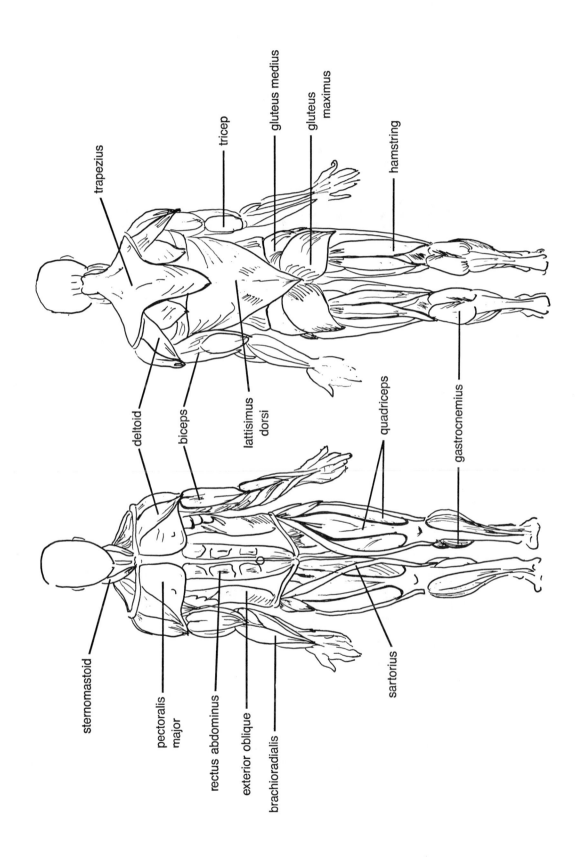

trapezius

tricep

gluteus medius

gluteus maximus

hamstring

deltoid

biceps

lattisimus dorsi

quadriceps

gastrocnemius

sternomastoid

pectoralis major

rectus abdominus

exterior oblique

brachioradialis

sartorius

LESSON 5

Imagery and Relaxing Phrases

BACKGROUND FOR THE TEACHER

The following lesson and tapes deal with imagery and relaxing phrases. The students will first try to imagine situations and feelings and then bodily sensations that may lead to actual physiological changes. If the children can hook into these images well enough, they should be able to produce these changes.

This is not just an idle hope. The mind and body are not two separate entities. Every cell is related structurally and functionally to every other cell, and our thoughts and feelings are ultimately connected to our bodies. Indeed, this is evident in anyone who has ingested caffeine, alcohol, tranquilizers, or any other chemical that affects both mental and physical function. There are other ways that we have seen the mind affect the body. When we get embarrassed, we blush. The emotional reaction causes the physical change. Under a lot of stress, people often look run down and may even seem to age more quickly. You may also have heard of "placebo" effects. This is where something neutral, which should not be capable of producing a change, causes a change simply because there had been an expectation of change. An example would be a person drinking colored water that he or she believed was a medicine.

Hypnosis is another way of working on the mind in order to affect the body. Scientific studies have demonstrated that behavior can be modified as a result of a hypnotic suggestion. Autogenic phrases that suggest heaviness, calmness, and warmth have also been shown to be able to bring about changes. The power of suggestion is certainly a phenomenon that each of us has experienced as well. "Mind over matter" is not just an expression.

As commonplace as the interaction between mind and body is, it seems to be in the realm of involuntary action. However, in recent years many things that were thought to be involuntary have been found to be able to be controlled. Biofeedback is a field that trains people to gain control over bodily processes that previously had been thought uncontrollable. People have been taught to control such "involuntary" functions as heartbeat, blood pressure, skin temperature, brain wave patterns, and muscle activity. The principle is that, by using machinery that can measure the function and give rapid feedback when it is increasing and decreasing, the person can discover what it takes, internally, to produce a change.

Note must be made here about the opposite phenomenon taking place. Some things we believe to be voluntary may become involuntary habitual patterns, so internalized that they are removed from conscious control and occur automatically. Held postural patterns are an example, as are areas of frozen muscle tension.

All of this has a direct relation to imagery. In trying to raise and lower hand temperature, for example, many people have tried to imagine their hand in a warm or cold situation, such as lying in the hot sun or reaching into an ice box. This can help start the temperature change and control. Some people may perform better when given slides and tape recordings suggesting heat or cold. In this case, the people had an image with which to work. It is possible that there are memories or images of these feelings of heat and cold and the bodily changes that accompany them. The people can go back in their memory for the "image" of the event and retrieve it.

The idea of images has been around for a long time. We are using images all the time. Vision is totally dependent on the use of images. The process of vision consists of a constant series of eye movements and fixations. This never stops. We never "look" at anything (fixate on it) for more than a fraction of a second. Even when we are "staring" at something, there is constant eye movement and fixating. There is almost no perception while the eye movements occur. During these movements we are dealing with the world solely through images, or memories. We have a memory trace of what was perceived during the fixation. During the eye movement, it is the memory trace that we are dealing with. In this way, the world looks like an uninterrupted whole rather than like a flickering old-time movie.

We are familiar with auditory (hearing) images as well. The "tip of the tongue" phenomenon, where we can almost feel the word, but can't quite retrieve it, is an example. We first will probably have a memory or image of the first letter or sound or even some other sound in the word. Later, the whole word comes to us. We may even have first thought of words that had similar sounds. There seem to have been images of the sounds.

Memory experts use images all the time. They work with similar sounds to try to couple pictures in their mind with the thing they are trying to remember. In Roman times, orators would use the following technique, utilizing images, in remembering a speech. They would imagine walking through a familiar house, and associate different parts of the house with different parts of the speech. They would then visualize walking through the house and "picking up" each part of the speech in the appropriate room.

Teachers often give students mnemonic devices to help them remember things. This is really just the use of a coding or auditory image.

Babies have no language but still learn many things. They must deal with the world completely from the point of view of the use of images—visual and auditory, as well as kinesthetic. They learn to recognize visual patterns, auditory sounds, and the kinesthetic cues that later allow them to learn to walk, ride a bicycle, ask for a toy, and hold a crayon.

In the same way that we have visual and auditory memories or images, there may also be kinesthetic images. This would be images of the "feel" of things. As we experience a heartbeat, change in hand temperature, muscle tightening or any other bodily change, we may have memories forming of the "feel." This may be occurring even though we are not really paying attention to these occurrences. We may, however, be able to use these images to help bring about the recurrence of the physiological occurrences. By working on the use of images, we may be able to help children become more adept at noting and visualizing changes in their bodies. They can then control these changes better.

Both the imagery and the autogenic tapes that follow this lesson try to do the same thing. They want to help the child to relax his or her body. If they do them correctly, they will slow down sympathetic nervous system activity. This is the nervous system that kicks in during the "fight or flight" stress-type responses.

The phrases used on Tape II, Side 1, Dialogue 5 are similar to the autogenic phrases introduced by Wolfgang Luthe and Johannes H. Schultz in *Autogenic Therapy, Volumes I-VI* (Orlando, Fla.: Grune & Stratton, 1969–1972). These have been found to do very well in helping people to achieve a relaxed state.

If children can really "feel" and produce the images of warmth in the hands, for example, they will have had to direct blood flow to the hands. They will have vasodilated. This is the opposite of the vasoconstriction of the blood vessels that occurs under stress. By changing breathing patterns, relaxing muscles, and slowing down sympathetic nervous system activity, the children are learning an entire response of relaxation.

LESSON 5

Purposes: To show the children that they use images all the time in their lives, and to show them the connection between the images in their minds and what happens to their bodies.

Materials Needed

Large, colorful object

Tape I, Side 2, Dialogue 4 and II, Side 1, Dialogue 5

Drawing paper (*optional*)

Crayons or colored pencils (*optional*)

Directions

1. Explain to the children that when they see things with their eyes, an image appears in their brain. This image is retained in the memory. To demonstrate this, have the children stare for 15 seconds at a large, colorful object you hold up. Tell students to try to remember the object. Now put the object away and have the children close their eyes and visualize the object. Ask questions about its size, shape, color, and other details. You might even ask the children to draw the object from memory.

2. Point out how everyone has the ability to go to their memories and produce images or pictures in their minds. This can be conceptualized as "seeing" without using the eyes. Explain how people use images when dreaming, and discuss the power of these images in creating emotional reactions. Most children will be able to describe an experience when the imagery of a dream created an emotional and a physiological change. For example, have the children ever awakened with a smile after a pleasant dream or in a sweat after a nightmare? Daydreams can produce the same reactions. You might even have the children try to daydream for a few minutes. Can they really "see" the image or "feel" an emotional reaction?

3. Continue this discussion on imagery; you might want to refer to the "Background for the Teacher" section to guide the children's understanding of how vision is actually the constant use of images.

4. Discuss how hypnosis and the power of suggestion rely upon the use of images. Many children will probably have an anecdote to contribute about hypnotism. Explain that when the power of suggestion leads to an actual physiological change, some type of imagery was used, although not necessarily a visual image. Placebo effects are a good example to use with the children. Give the following definition:

A placebo effect is a change that occurs as a result of something that shouldn't be able to cause the change.

An example of this might be if a person were given colored water and told that it was a drug that induces laughter, and then that person began to laugh.

Explain that the placebo effect has been suggested as the reason why some unscientific remedies for illnesses seemed to have worked at times.

5. Discuss some of the points in the "Background for the Teacher" section about auditory images and the "tip-of-the-tongue" phenomenon. Most children will have experienced this.

6. Discuss how people can have kinesthetic, or "feeling," images. A good example to use is riding a bicycle. You can't say exactly what you learned to do correctly, but you know that you now have the "feel" of how to do it. The same is true in many sports—you have an image of how it feels to do things correctly. Baseball, bowling, and golf are a few examples of this.

Ask if anyone can wiggle their ears or move their eyebrows in an unusual way. Point out that these people have paid attention to gaining control of a bodily function that most of us have not tried to control or have not tried hard enough to learn. Explain how biofeedback can help people to learn to control bodily functions thought to be involuntary. Remind the students that they all know how thoughts can affect the body because they all have seen someone else blush or have blushed themselves. Most children will also be able to identify with the idea that thinking about a scary movie or a bully can cause them to feel fear all over again, and, likewise, that thinking about a sad event can cause them to feel sad and perhaps cry.

This discussion serves as an introduction to the tapes on imagery and on warm and relaxing feelings. Both of these tapes depend on the children's ability to visualize images and feelings. Point out that in just the same way that we can get scared and upset by thinking of scary and upsetting things, we can also become calm, relaxed, peaceful, and happy by thinking pleasant thoughts.

Emphasize that this is a difficult task, and that to get the kinds of bodily changes we want, it is necessary for the students to take the tapes seriously, concentrate very hard, and really try to imagine the things they are asked to. Also mention that it may take several listenings before they are able to experience the feeling.

7. Play Tape I, Side 2, Dialogue 4. (The dialogue follows this lesson.)
8. Play Tape II, Side 1, Dialogue 5. (The dialogue follows this lesson.)

Follow-up Suggestions

After having asked the children to produce vivid yet calm images, you might ask the children to draw their visualized scenes. They can illustrate the calm place or the helpful person they imagined, or just draw a picture showing what the relaxation exercise suggests to them. Keep a folder of these drawings on display, or exhibit them in the classroom.

TAPE I, SIDE 2, DIALOGUE 4

On this tape we're going to use our imagination. Everybody always tells you to use your imagination when you make up a story, so you've certainly done it before. In order to use your imagination, you have to go into your memory of things that you know. Even when you make something up you had to have something in your head to go back to. For example, suppose you wrote a story and made up your own imaginary land with crazy mixed-up animals that breathed out ice cream and had four eyes and green fur. You still had to go back into your memory to know that animals breathe and that they have fur and eyes and that there is something called ice cream. So when I say to use your imagination and feel things or picture things, I mean to go back in your memory to really remember what they looked like, felt like, or smelled like. At first, I'll help you out by supplying some suggestions and some sounds that may help remind you of the experience. Later on, I'll want you to try to do it by yourself. Okay, let's go.

First just imagine that you're writing your name on a piece of paper. Picture your hand moving and holding the pencil. Now picture walking to school. See if you can feel how your legs feel as they move. Picture the sun on you or the wind in your hair.

Now I want you to try to picture yourself out in the woods. You just found a little stream with a waterfall and you've sat down next to it. Try to picture the stream with the water flowing. Each of you has seen different streams so you'll all probably be seeing different pictures in your mind. Some of you may never have seen a stream except on television. It doesn't matter. Just imagine the one that you can remember. Picture the water. Listen to the sound of the water. Okay, here's one for those of you who live in the city. We're going to imagine a traffic jam. You've all been in one or seen one on television or in a movie. You should try to hear the horns. Picture the cars. Imagine the looks on the faces of the people in the cars and on the street.

All right, one more exercise before we get to the hard stuff. I'm going to give you a few situations or things to think about. When I say so, try to really picture each. It's not easy, but try to remember the looks, sounds, smells, feel, and tastes that go along with the experience. Here's the first. It's July 4th and people are shooting off firecrackers, lots of them and all at once. Sit back and see, hear and smell it. Don't touch, though. Now I want you to think of the prettiest, nicest-smelling flowers that you can think of. See if you can bring back the memory of what they looked and smelled like. This is hard, I know, but try to do it. Don't just sit there and pretend to be trying. *TRY!* If you're having trouble remembering, don't get discouraged. Just keep trying and you'll get better at it.

Now it's your turn to really go back into your own mind and look for a memory. That's what we're doing, you know. We're looking for memories. You have them. If you had something really nice or bad happen, it's probably there in your mind. You just have to track it down. Let's start with an easy one. Think of the best food smell that you can think of. Maybe it's also your favorite food to eat and you can imagine what it tastes like too. Think hard. Picture the kitchen, or a plate of it, or holding it up to your mouth. Try to remember the smells and tastes. Is it pizza, steak, Chinese food, apple pie? Whatever it is, try to imagine it.

Now for just a minute try to think of something that smells bad—rotten eggs, sweaty socks, skunk, anything. Can you find that memory? It's there.

Okay, now to what this is all about, your body. I want you to do the same thing that you've been doing. Go back in your memory. If I ask you to feel warm, think about

Tape I, Side 2, Dialogue 4, continued

something warm and how you felt. It could be the sun beating down on you at the beach, a campfire, or sitting next to a radiator. Try to remember how your body felt then and make it feel that way again. Make it feel warm.

Let's start out by getting into a comfortable position. All set? We're going to begin with a couple of breathing exercises. Begin your deep, slow breathing. As you breathe in, I want you to think of the number one. Not only should you think of the number one, but try to imagine the number one floating in space in front of you. As you breathe out, you will think of the number one and imagine a huge block number one floating in front of you. Then you will breathe in and think of two and out while you still think of two. We'll continue this up until five. Keep your eyes closed as you do this so that you can really imagine those numbers floating out in front of you. When we get to five, we're going to count backwards to one and then stop. All right now, begin with one. Inhale. Now exhale on one. Inhale, two. Breathe out, two. In on three. Out on three. Inhale on four. Exhale on four. Take a last slow breath in on five and breathe out on five. Now inhale on five. Exhale on five. Breathe in on four, and out on four. Now in again on three, and out on three. Inhale on two, and out on two. In on one, and out on one. Good. Now try to stay as relaxed as you can.

Scan your muscles now and let any tight ones just loosen up and relax. Let them hang loose and calm. Let each breath exhale any new tension you feel.

Now picture yourself lying on a cloud. Imagine one like you would see in a cartoon. Picture yourself way up above the ground, as high as a plane, and floating down. As you go down, imagine yourself feeling a little calmer, as you get low enough to see beautiful birds flying nearby.

As you slowly float down some more, try to feel a change so that you feel a little more relaxed by the time you get to the level of the treetops. Picture a beautiful kite floating next to you. Go on now and try to feel a little calmer, more relaxed, and better as you near the ground. Take a nice, slow ride to the ground and try to really feel just a little calmer than you were at the treetops. You may feel heavy in your arms and legs, and that's good. They also may begin to feel warm. That's good too. Keep breathing deeply.

As you get to the ground, you are to imagine that you see yourself in a calm, beautiful day. You are outdoors in a beautiful spot. Imagine your favorite outdoor place. There may be green grass, a lake, a waterfall, a perfect sky. The sun is warm and you feel it warm your skin. Walk over to a comfortable spot and lie down. Breathe deeply and release tension. Breathe in the warm, fresh air and feel the sun warming your body, especially your hands. The sun's warmth can warm you inside too. You feel bright and warm inside. Try to feel it going through your blood, warming your body. Feel at peace. Breathe away any tension you feel. This is how good your inner person can feel. Remember it so that you can come back to this feeling again. You can come back to this calm feeling whenever you want. Every time you practice relaxing you can get better at finding this place and this feeling. The feeling can get even warmer and the sun can get even brighter.

While you feel this way, try to think about how good you feel. Think about how good you are for doing positive things for yourself, like relaxing. You will get better and better the more you practice, just like with anything else.

Feel the energy around you. You have a lot of healing energy. You can use it to make things feel better that may be bothering you. If you have an ache or problem

Tape I, Side 2, Dialogue 4, continued

anywhere in your body, imagine warm, healing energy moving there and making it feel better.

Now imagine yourself floating off. You may see yourself rolling over onto a magic carpet or a hot-air balloon, or even just lifting yourself up on your own, but imagine floating up higher into the sky now. You are getting even more of the sun's warming rays and should be able to feel even more of the warm glow as you get higher up. Float away. Now slowly float down to where you were. As you near the ground, you are to picture a person waiting to greet you. It may be someone you know or a wonderful stranger. Picture this person as your helper. If you want to relax, you can always imagine this person here. It will be a smiling person who will be there to help you feel calm and solve your problems.

It is safe as you land. Feel the warmth in your quiet spot. Feel the warmth of this person as they take your hand and lead you out of the clearing. Remember, you can always come back here to this beautiful, calm spot and you can always find this person.

Once more, now, just feel the warmth in your arms and hands. Imagine the blood flowing through your arms bringing this warmth. Now slowly open your eyes. Slowly move your arms and legs and slowly come out of this relaxed state.

TAPE II, SIDE 1, DIALOGUE 5
(relaxing phrases)

We're going to start off with a short breathing exercise before anything else. You are going to take a deep, slow breath in and slowly count to five as you do this. You will hold it for four counts and then exhale for eight counts. If you can't hold your inhale or exhale for that whole time, just do the best you can. Try it now. In 2, 3, 4, 5…hold 2, 3, 4…Exhale 2, 3, 4, 5, 6, 7, 8. Good. Now do the same thing, but as you exhale you will make a hissing sound, like the letter "S." All right, inhale 2, 3, 4, 5…hold 2, 3, 4…breathe out with an "S" sound 3, 4, 5, 6, 7, 8. Good.

You are going to try to get your body to feel certain calming sensations now. You are going to try to imagine your body feeling the way that I suggest.

First of all, get in a good position for this. Sit up in your chair and hold your head straight up. Rest your feet on the floor, but out a little, not right under you. Rest your hands on your legs, a little above the knees. Now let your head just drop straight down so that your chin touches your chest. If you have room to do this lying down, you can put a pillow under your neck and knees and spread your arms and legs out a little bit away from your body.

When you do these exercises, don't try too hard. You are trying to relax, so if you get upset, you ruin the whole purpose. Now just let your thoughts flow in and out of your head. If a thought comes in, pretend that it came through your skin—from the outside—and that it just floats through your head and out through your skin on the other side.

Okay, let's begin. Close your eyes. Go back to your breathing first. Say to yourself three times: My breathing is calm and slow. Okay, say it to yourself—my breathing is calm and slow. My breathing is calm and slow. My breathing is calm and slow. Now say to

Tape II, Side 1, Dialogue 5, continued

yourself, also three times, I am getting relaxed. Say it to yourself. I am getting relaxed. I am getting relaxed. I am getting relaxed. Try to feel calm and peaceful and say to yourself (I won't even say it this time), I am calm and peaceful. Go ahead now.

Now you're going to concentrate on parts of your body. Concentrate on one arm now. If you're a righty, make it your right arm. If you're a lefty, your left one. First I want you to try to picture it feeling heavy, really heavy. If you could make it feel like it weighed 200 pounds and you couldn't even lift it, that would be perfect. Say to yourself and try to feel this: My arm is heavy. My arm is heavy. My arm is heavy. Now your other arm. Concentrate on it and feel it get heavy. Say to yourself, My arm is heavy. Say it to yourself two more times now. Keep your breathing slow and regular and deep all through this.

Let's go to the legs now. This time I want you to imagine that your legs just got filled with cement. Say to yourself, My right leg is heavy. Okay, say it: My right leg is heavy. Again, and feel it. One more time to yourself. Now your left leg. Feel that cement weighing it down. Say it with me now: My left leg is heavy. My left leg is heavy. My left leg is heavy. Now concentrate on both feet at once. Picture the cement oozing down to your feet and say to yourself three times, my feet are heavy. Go ahead, three times now. Now higher up to your stomach and abdomen. Say to yourself and really feel it right after I say it now. My stomach is heavy and relaxed and quiet. Say it to yourself now three times. Up a little higher now. My neck and shoulders are heavy. Say it to yourself, My neck and shoulders are heavy. Again, and again.

Now that everything feels heavy, we want them also to feel warm. Just two times for each now. First, your arms. When you say, My arms are warm, try to feel the warmth. Think of nice warm water all around them warming up. Okay, say it to yourself. My arms are warm. My arms are warm. Concentrate on your right one. My right arm is warm. And now the left one. My left arm is warm. Move it to your hands. They are in nice warm water too. My arms and hands are warm. My arms and hands are warm. Your legs again now. My right leg is warm. Feel it stepping into a tub of warm water or feel the warm sun beating down on it. My right leg is warm. Now picture the left leg stepping in as warm water surrounds it. My left leg is warm. My left leg is warm. Now say this to yourself and imagine it: Warmth is flowing into my legs. Warmth is flowing into my legs. And back to your arms: Warmth is flowing into my arms. Warmth is flowing into my arms. Keep your breathing calm and slow. Picture your heart now as you say, My heartbeat is calm and even. My heartbeat is calm and even. Now up higher as you say to yourself, My neck and jaw and forehead are relaxed. Concentrate on your forehead. Picture it smooth, no wrinkles. Erase any wrinkles as you say to yourself, My forehead is smooth. My forehead is smooth. Now let your forehead feel relaxed still, but also cool, like someone has a cool, damp cloth on it. Say to yourself, My forehead is cool and relaxed. My forehead is cool and relaxed. We are going to be finishing up, so start concentrating on your mind and let it feel awake and alert, not sleepy. And say to yourself, I am alert and aware. I am alert and awake. Feel good all over and say to yourself, I feel relaxed. I feel relaxed. Now begin to feel even more alert and say to yourself, I feel refreshed. I am refreshed. Breathe deeply now. Move your arms and legs just a bit, just to begin to get them ready to get up. Open your eyes and slowly sit up straight. Make all movements slowly and feel refreshed, alert and relaxed. Feel good.

LESSON 6

Movement Awareness

BACKGROUND FOR THE TEACHER

The previous lessons have offered relaxation techniques that seek to calm and regulate the autonomic nervous system. Movement awareness, or neuromuscular reeducation, represents another method of controlling physical behavior. Movement awareness leads to greater physical awareness, which helps one to recognize and release muscular tension that can interfere with proper physical and mental functioning. The most familiar techniques are the Alexander technique, Feldenkrais techniques (awareness-through-movement classes and functional integration), Kinetic Awareness, and Ideokinesis. The benefits of these methods are

- Release of muscular tension
- Improved posture
- Increased range and efficiency of movement
- Greater sense of well-being
- Enhanced self-image
- Increased physical and mental awareness

The originators of these techniques had physical problems that were not improved by traditional means. In the process of curing their disabilities, which included vocal problems, a knee injury, and severe osteoarthritis, each came to the same conclusion—growing up and adapting to the environment causes a buildup of muscle tension. Furthermore, rigid muscle patterns interfere with the proper functioning of our bodies. They found that many physical ailments, disabilities, and injuries were not solely the result of accidents, personality, or heredity, but were also due to continuous interference with the body's natural functioning.

Essentially, the originators of movement techniques saw the human body as an efficiently designed structure. The skeleton distributes and transfers weight throughout the body and acts against the force of gravity with a complex lever system. The muscles are designed to move the bones and assist in the response to gravity. Therefore, good posture is based on a specific weight-bearing relationship. When this relationship is maintained, it takes little effort to stand up, and simple movement requires no excess effort. A good movement is smooth, and generally takes a path that the bones would take if attached only by ligaments. There should be no need to make shifts or adjustments before moving.

Muscles communicate information about their position and movement, so we always know where we are in space without visual assistance. The ability to sense and act on feedback from the muscles helps us make changes in posture and gauge the amount of effort needed for movement. Movement teachers refer to our muscle sense as *kinesthetic*.

If the body is continually held in one position, problems occur. Excess tension interferes with proper circulation. The waste product called lactic acid then builds up and can cause discomfort. Holding muscles also makes them stiff and inflexible. In addition, the distribution of weight is usually disturbed. When the muscles are held out of their natural alignment, they must do work they are not designed for, such as support weight. This causes stress on the muscles and wear and tear on the joints. More effort is needed to move held areas. Furthermore, excess muscular effort dulls a person's ability to get feedback from the muscles, and the result is to respond with more tension.

When the body is further stressed by physical activity, injury can result. If a person runs or jumps without proper weight distribution, injury to joints may occur. Two common areas of injury are the lower back and knees, two major weight-transference areas.

There are many causes of poor physical awareness and inappropriate muscular tension. They include

- Genetic factors, illness, injury, poor nutrition
- Poor adaptation to physical environment
- Culturally learned ideas about how the body works and what it can do
- Imitation of others
- Psychological factors
- Vocational factors

The human infant must learn all his or her physical responses. The process of learning, which is usually by trial and error, is colored by many factors. For example, when a child makes it across the room unassisted, walking is usually considered successful. However, the child (urged on by eager parents), may have walked before the hip joints were completely developed (which comes from crawling), or may have already picked up the faulty gait of one parent. The child may also have emotional stress connected with the act of walking (the anxiety of trying to please parents or a fall associated with the activity), but if the walking is reinforced and repeated, it will become habit and feel natural, no matter how disturbed it is.

Emotion is another strong contributor to the development of muscle patterns and sensitivity. All strong emotions—fear, anxiety, depression—have a corresponding physical pattern. The response to fear mentioned in Lesson 1 involves muscle contraction. Research has shown this response to be a stereotypical response and includes tensing and rounding the shoulders, thrusting the neck forward, straightening the arms, contracting the chest, flexing the knees, and holding the breath. If the response occurs often enough, the individual will not release the muscle pattern, and that posture will become habitual.

Indeed, movement researchers have shown that by the time a child reaches the age of ten, he or she may already have accumulated muscle tension that is not released and interferes with movement.

Our society's adaptation to chairs further contributes to poor posture and poor kinesthetic sense. When the child enters school, he or she must conform to certain regulations that may interfere with physical development. The child must learn to shift her or his attention from the body to the mind. In order to sit still for long hours, the child must ignore physical distress signals from the body. Continued blocking of physical cues distorts a person's ability to truly feel the body. In addition, chairs and desks do not always conform to the child's structure. The normal position for work is to be slumped over the desk, back curved, neck forward, shoulders hunched, and hand cramped while writing. This position involves effort and excess contraction of the back muscles. When the child stands, the weak stomach muscles cannot support a balanced position. The result is often a swayed back. The slumped position, however, will eventually come to feel normal. The child will slump in front of the television for hours outside of the classroom and, as the muscle pattern becomes fixed, any other position will feel uncomfortable.

By the time a person reaches maturity, he or she may have, for many reasons, accumulated many poor muscle habits, such as curved neck, rounded shoulders, swayed back, locked and rotated knees, shallow breathing, and a poor body sense. The person may assume it is genetic and unchangeable, but it is a learned habit; it can be changed.

John Dewey talks about the problem of changing poor postural habits in *Human Nature and Conduct*. He notes that the current belief is that poor posture is merely the result of not doing something right, and that one merely needs to be told or to tell oneself to stand up straight to achieve that end. However, he points out that standing improperly is actually a powerful habit. As long as the conditions that formed the habit are present, the poor posture will persist. If a person works at standing correctly, Dewey points out, he may be standing differently but it will only be a different type of poor standing, partly because he does not know what standing correctly really feels like. Dewey later solved his own problem of poor postural habits through the body work of F. M. Alexander, whom he frequently wrote about.

NOTE: For more information on movement awareness and the different techniques, see the bibliography at the end of this book.

LESSON 6

Purpose: To show and explain to the children that they do not always feel what is happening within their bodies and that this interferes with their ability to use their bodies healthfully.

Materials Needed

Workbook Activities 6-1 and 6-2

Tape II, Side 1, Dialogue 6

Directions

1. Ask the students if they can describe how *any* part of their body feels at that moment. If there is a response, it will probably be about an ache or pain or something negative. If there is no answer, start a discussion on how often the only time a person is usually asked to describe how the body feels is when he or she is hurt or sick. People don't usually have a chance to pay attention to what feels healthy. As a result, only negative feelings are described.

Introduce words, such as "tight," "loose," "mobile," "warm," and "open" that might describe feelings in the body. Ask the children to suggest good feelings.

2. Explain that one reason we don't really pay attention to our bodies is that we seem to always be doing a movement the same way or sitting in the same manner. This way then starts to feel normal. However, the normal way is not always the best or even most natural way.

Poor posture will come to feel good even though it is not proper. Why? People develop bad posture and poor use of their bodies for many reasons. Explain these reasons to the children, using the "Background for the Teacher" section and the following information as your guide.

Explain that we have to learn all of our movement responses and give examples of how they can be interfered with. We copy our parents when we learn such early skills as standing or walking. Our parents may have problems themselves, or they may teach us incorrectly, or we may imitate their incorrect style.

Emotion is another reason. All emotion has a physical result. We become tense when we are afraid, for example, and may not release the tension once the fear is gone. Make a point of this by letting the children show how they would hold themselves if they were afraid. Have them note their posture, breathing, muscle tension, and so on.

Continue to explain that we must also learn to conform to social situations, which is another reason for improper use of the body. Although this conformity is necessary at school, problems can occur. Sitting for long periods of time dulls the ability to pay attention to the body, and the chosen position is usually incorrect. The slumped, rounded position children sit in weakens posture and increases tension. As the teacher, you know how difficult it is to conduct a large class without the discipline of seating. However, you can add movement breaks to release the students' tensions. Ask the children to close their eyes and quietly stretch their bodies. Have them really pay attention to the body and move what needs to stretch. This is a good way to reinforce what is being learned through this program and helps give release from the long and unnatural periods of stillness.

3. Ask how many children feel they have good control of their bodies. Can they move all body parts separately? Have them try moving the spine at the middle of the rib cage to the left, without moving the stomach. See who can flare out his or her nostrils. Let them try to move the fingers of both hands (without any hesitation) to each of the following positions. (You may want to demonstrate the positions first.)

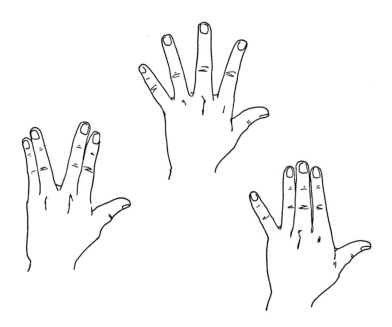

Let the children try to move the shoulder joint without actively using any arm muscles. They should move the shoulder up, back, down, and then release forward. The neck and other shoulder should remain stationary.

Because many students will have difficulty with these movements, the point should come out that most people do not have great control over most of their body, mainly because they do not pay attention to it. Inform the students that if they become aware of their body and *sense* it, they will find out what is wrong. To keep the body healthy, it must move in as many directions as it will go, often, *and with no strain.*

Explain that movement should be slow and deliberate in order to feel what is happening. It is like using a magnifying glass to show up the problems. The students should try to work the muscles that surround a joint.

4. Play Tape II, Side 1, Dialogue 6. (The dialogue follows this lesson.)

Follow-up Suggestions

1. You may want to talk a bit about posture and what good posture entails. Ask students to show some good postures. Notice the stiffness associated with posture. Ask each demonstrator to see if he or she can drop the shoulders (most will hold them too high). If you notice anything very wrong, tell the child so that he or she can correct it and let go. The position should not be held. Explain that it is not good to hold any position too tightly or for too long, even if it is a good position. The more students become aware of their bodies and release the holding, the closer to their natural alignment they will get.

2. Refer to the standing posture diagram (see Activity 6-1) in the workbook. Have the children notice the line of gravity and the relationship of body parts.

Remind students that good posture requires little effort and should allow smooth movement in any direction at any moment without having to adjust first. There should be no strain on muscles.

3. The following sitting posture is designed to give the children a sense of correct posture when they are sitting in a chair. Have them sit forward in the chair with their feet on the floor. The spine should be straight, but not rigid or stiffly held. Have them slowly move slightly forward and backward in order to get a sense of feeling the "sitting bones" (ischia). They should do it until they really get a feeling for being on top of those bones. When sitting directly over these bones, the body is balanced and little effort is needed to hold it up. Refer the students to the sitting posture diagrams (Activity 6-2) in the workbook.

**TAPE II, SIDE 1, DIALOGUE 6
(MOVEMENT AWARENESS—SHOULDERS/ARMS)**

This tape is designed to help you to better understand how it feels to move only one muscle group at a time. All of the movements that you perform will be very, very small. Also, the movements that you do will be very slow—maybe slower than you ever thought you could move or wanted to move. We will move slowly in order to let you feel the muscles as they move and to learn how much effort is needed to move them. Most of us use more energy or tension than is really necessary for any given motion. I would like you to act like detectives by looking for clues in the muscles, bones, and tissues, places you may never have thought to look before. Our watchwords will be *small* and *slow*. Remember, it is easy to do a big, fast movement, but very difficult to do a small, slow one. You will be acquiring a new skill and gaining more control and awareness of your body.

I would like you to get comfortable. Sit back in your chair. If your feet do not rest on the floor, sit forward in the chair, tall but not stiff. Place your hands in your lap. I'd like you to think of your head as filled with helium, like a balloon. It should float easily on top of your body, feeling light and free. The neck muscles should be relaxed, but your neck should sit tall, with your chin pointing downward. Think forward and downward with your chin, up with your neck. Now please close your eyes and sense how your body feels right now. Notice your neck...your shoulders...Is there any part that feels tight? Is any area strained?

Tape II, Side 1, Dialogue 6, continued

I'd also like you to notice your breathing. Keep your eyes closed. Where is the air coming in? Is it your nose or your mouth? What is the speed? I would like you to try to slow down your breathing. Do this by feeling calm and by filling your belly slowly with air. Let it fill your whole torso, up to your chest. Let the air out slowly, letting as much out as you can without forcing. Continue breathing slowly and deeply on your own. Good. Try to remember how the deep breathing felt, and every once in a while take in a nice, slow breath.

Today we are going to work on our shoulders. Before we begin, I would like you to loosen the neck. I'd like you to move your head very slowly to the right only about an inch, then come back to center. Do that now. Now move the same distance to the left and back. Good. Let's make the movement smooth between the two directions. It is only a small movement. Go ahead. Now let's add another inch on each side. Make the movement smooth. Remember to keep your chin down. Keep moving. Keep adding movement to the side. You may feel that it is difficult to move so little a distance, particularly slowly. You may even feel your muscles twitch a little, as if they wanted to move more. Just ignore that and keep trying. Be sure to keep your jaw and mouth loose and relaxed. Keep your mouth open just slightly as you move. I hope you've been moving to each side. Now go as far to each side as possible. Good. I'd like you to try to keep your neck relaxed as we work now on the shoulders.

Please put your left hand on the front of your right shoulder, just above the arm pit. Feel around the area gently to feel the bones and muscles. With your fingers still there, move your shoulder forward about one-half inch and then back to center. Good. A half inch isn't much movement, but it's an important difference in your body. Let's do that again.

Now take away your hand and put it in your lap. Keep your eyes closed and move your shoulder again, forward and back. Do it with me...Forward...and back to center...Forward...and back. You will continue on your own. As you move I would like you to sense what your shoulder feels like. What do the muscles feel like? Keep moving...slowly...forward...and back. As you move, try to make your movements lighter by using less effort. Very good. Now place your right hand on your left shoulder. Move it slowly, forward and back. Repeat that. Now rest your hand in your lap and slowly move the left shoulder forward and back to center. With me—forward...and back...forward...and back. Does the left side feel the same as the right side? If it is different, notice how different. Keep moving slowly...forward...and back to center at this speed. Forward and back. Make sure the right shoulder is not moving and all other muscles are relaxed as much as possible. Continue; very good. Now open your eyes for a moment and rest.

I'd like to combine some directions now. You will lift your right shoulder straight up, then move it straight back, and then let it slide down slowly. You will be making the top of a box. Remember to move gently, slowly and smoothly. Try it with me now. Up...back...down...slide forward...up...back...down...slide forward...up... back...down...slide forward. Let your shoulder slide forward before you start up again. Now try it on your own.... That was very good. Now I'd like you to explore all the directions that your shoulder can go...up...down...side...back...diagonal...any way that you want...smoothly. Try to go as slowly as possible and smoothly and continuously. I'll bet we've got some speed demons out there! Keep doing it now, anyway it can move. Slowly, remember. Now I want you to rest for a moment and sense what your shoulder

Tape II, Side 1, Dialogue 6, continued

feels like. Do you remember how it felt before? Does it feel the same now? Does it feel the same as the left? Let's use the left shoulder and make the same box... up...back...down. Remember to make angles instead of circles. Please do it with me...Up...back...down. Slide forward. Slide forward. Up...back...down... up...back...down. Slide forward. Now proceed on your own. Good.

Now move the left shoulder smoothly in all the directions it will go. Be creative, but please go slowly. Keep going smoothly. Good. Now move both shoulders together. Still slowly and smoothly, but experimenting. Now open your eyes.

We are going to use the arm and the shoulders now. Let your right arm hang at the side and notice how it feels. Really pay attention to your arm. Then raise it slowly to the side of you about two inches and let it come back slowly. Rest. Now do this again, but raise it about five or six inches, and back down. Really let it hang freely when it comes back down. Now I'd like you to raise it all the way to the ear, slowly. Try to keep your shoulder down. When you've gone high enough that your arm has reached your ear, slowly lower the arm back down. Good. Let's do that again. Let your arm, the wrist, and elbow be as relaxed as possible. This time as you go up, I want you to add a little bounce—just a little pulse. Try that now. Good. A little bounce now. Let's do it one more time. Okay. Let your arm hang at the side. How does it feel? Now we're going to do the left arm. Slowly raise it about two inches and then lower it. Now let's move upward a little further. Good. Slowly lower it. Now let's move all the way to the ear again. Don't cheat by moving the head to the arm. Keep the shoulder down and the arm relaxed. And now come back down. Let's do that again. Let your arm hang after you come down. This time let's add the tiny bounces up and down. Good. Now, one last time.

Okay, now sense how your shoulders feel. Do they feel any different than when you started? Let's just shrug them and move them around a bit. Do a few little circles. Remember, it is excellent for your body to move, and little movements can loosen and relax you. Feel good.

Name _____   ACTIVITY 6–1

Date _____

The Spine

DIRECTIONS: Become familiar with the names of the bones of the spine. Then look at yourself in a full-length mirror. Do you have correct posture?

The Spine **Proper Skeletal-Muscular Alignment**
(the correct way to stand up straight)

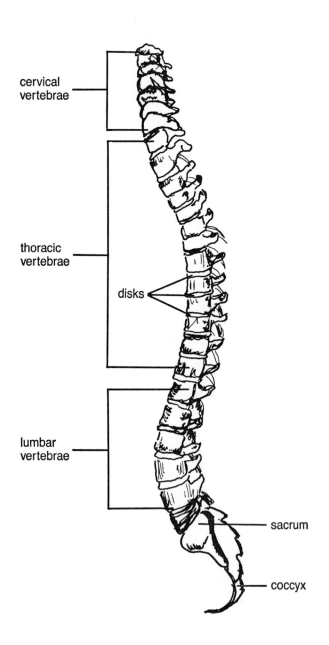

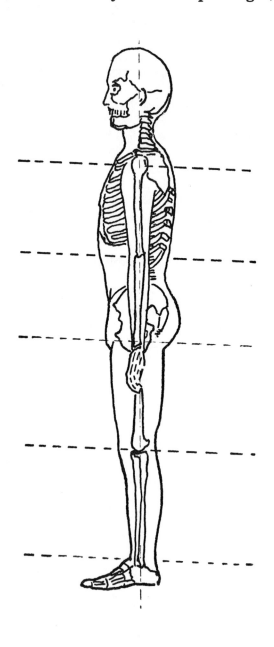

© 1986 by The Center for Applied Research in Education, Inc.

Posture

DIRECTIONS: Become aware of how you are sitting as you read this. Are you sitting correctly or incorrectly?

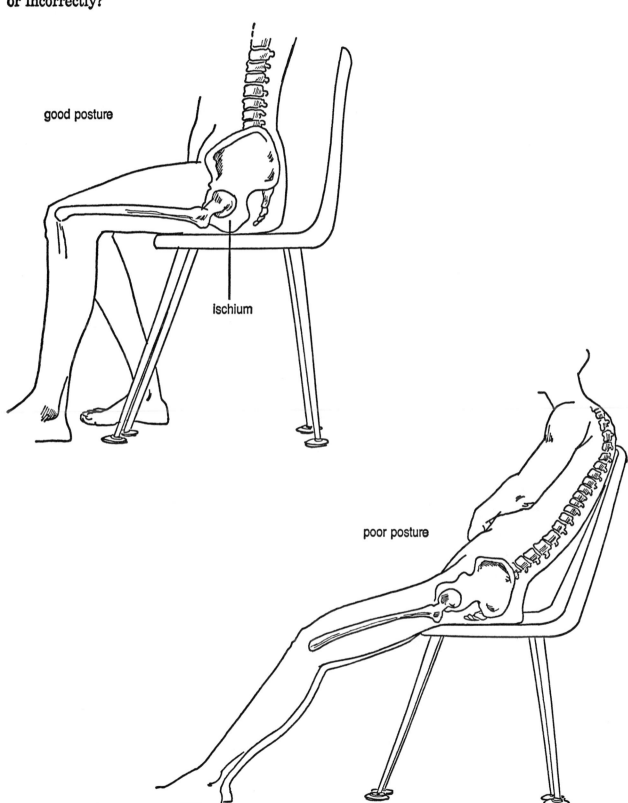

good posture

ischium

poor posture

LESSON 7

Physical Fitness

BACKGROUND FOR THE TEACHER

Physical exercise is one method of helping a person to feel better and is an important element in any stress reduction program. Exercise has been shown to not only improve the body's functioning but to improve one's mood, relieve nervous tension, and help fight depression and insomnia. Good physical fitness means having enough energy to meet daily demands on the body easily and having energy left over for recreational activities and any emergency that might arise.

Human beings were meant to be active. In order for the body to function properly it must engage in some form of physical activity. Exercise helps the heart to pump blood and promotes a better exchange of gases in the lungs and tissues. Indeed, all our bodily systems function through and need movement.

Yet, modern people lead a comparatively inactive life. The fight or flight response to fear is a preparation for physical action, yet today the response rarely ends in physical activity. Modern living has taken away almost all necessity for physical activity; therefore we must create time in our lives for exercise.

Exercise involves working the muscles beyond what is normally demanded of them. However, this can be very specific. Some exercises develop strength, others flexibility, and still others endurance. A good exercise program includes all three types. Exercises that develop balance, coordination, and speed are also important, especially for children.

Activities should be judged on the basis of their contribution to a total fitness program. Running, for example, develops muscular and cardiovascular endurance, but not strong arms. Weight lifting develops muscular strength, but not endurance. And, whereas golf and doubles tennis are excellent recreational activities, they do not improve physical fitness to any great degree.

Let us now define a few terms.

Strength: This refers to the amount of force we can exert or weight we can lift. Strength is developed by contracting the muscles either isotonically or isometrically. Isotonic exercise involves lengthening the muscle through movement, whereas there is no movement in the isometric, or held, contraction. Calisthenics, push-ups, sit-ups, and weight training (isotonic) are good ways to strengthen muscles and build muscle mass. They are most effective when used in combination with flexibility exercises and endurance training.

Muscle Endurance: In order to sustain an activity your muscles must have endurance. This is developed through the repeated use of the muscles in low-resistance activities. (Resistance means working against weight; heavy weight training is a high-resistance exercise.) Cycling, jumping rope, and running are good ways of developing muscle endurance.

Flexibility: This is the measure of stretch or degree of motion in your muscles, tendons, ligaments, and joints. Since vigorous physical exercise hardens and tightens the muscles, making them more susceptible to strain and injury, it is important to keep the muscles as flexible as possible. Furthermore, a flexible muscle is stronger than a rigid one. You should stretch before and after any exercise activity, and stretching exercises should be an integral part of an exercise regimen. Yoga is an excellent means of gaining flexibility, and some forms of dance, especially ballet and modern, concentrate on lengthening and stretching the muscles.

Warm-up: You should always warm up before any exercise. Warm-up should not be just your stretching exercises, which also cause the muscles to contract. A good warm-up routine gently moves the joints and muscles in all the directions they can go without stress. Warming up increases the blood supply, raises the temperature and makes the muscles more pliable. Going slowly allows you to find out how your body feels before you work it. A gentle head roll that starts small and builds up is a good example of warming up. Then rotate the shoulders and arms. After all areas have been moved, you can begin stretching. After some stretching, then you will be ready to slowly begin your activity. Going slowly at first will let the muscles get ready for the increased demands to come. Taking time to warm up and stretch can greatly improve your performance and reduce the chance of injury or strain.

Cardiovascular Endurance: This refers to the ability of the heart and lungs to provide fuel to sustain activity. The term "aerobic exercise" is applied to any exercise that creates a sustained increase in oxygen demand. Fitness experts agree that in order to be truly physically fit, you must do some type of endurance or aerobic exercise. Endurance exercise begins to work at what is called the "training level," which is the point at which the heart is working at 70 to 85 percent of its maximum rate (the fastest the heart can beat and still pump blood to the body). You must do this about four times a week, or every other day, in the beginning. Once you become "trained," three thirty-minute sessions a week should be enough to maintain fitness. Running, swimming, and cycling are all good aerobic exercises. Swimming is excellent, because it places little strain on the bones and joints and uses various muscle groups. Running is good because you do not need a special place to do it.

The acknowledged benefits of regular endurance exercise (called the "training effect") include:

1. Improved efficiency of the heart (the heart increases in size and strength and the volume of blood pumped is increased)
2. Lower blood pressure
3. Increased utilization of oxygen in the system
4. Improved utilization of blood glucose
5. Reduction of body fat
6. Increased energy
7. Reduction of tension
8. Improved physical ability
9. Possible decrease in risk of heart disease
10. Enhanced sense of well-being

Many long-distance runners talk about a sense of intoxication they get from running. Indeed, studies have shown that endurance exercises can greatly affect your mood. *The Sportsmedicine Book* by Gabe Mirkin and Marshall Hoffman (Boston: Little, Brown and Co., 1978) relates clinical studies that found even mild exercise to be more relaxing than a tranquilizer. Some scientists believe this is due to the release of hormones from the brain. Certain studies have found increased levels of endorphins (considered to be the body's own tranquilizer) in the bloodstream. Others have measured increased levels of norepinephrine, which aids nerve transmission. Other mental benefits are improved alertness as a result of increased supply of oxygen to the brain and an increase in the ability to achieve deep sleep. Sticking to a regular exercise program also gives a person a sense of accomplishment.

Most stress experts believe exercise should be aerobic, rhythmic, and devoid of competition in order to be successful in reducing stress.

Many people want to know how much exercise is enough. The answer, of course, depends on what you want to achieve. Touching your toes five minutes a day or ten minutes of aerobic dance is not enough to lose weight or improve your heart. On the other hand, three half-hour aerobic dance classes a week have been shown to help in fighting depression and anxiety and in losing weight. Running eight to ten miles a week may be enough to begin to transform hard-driving type-A behavior into more easygoing type B (although we must realize that some people make sports and exercise a compulsion). Light exercise has proven to be successful in preventing loss of calcium in the bones, which could lead to osteoporosis. One can, however, get too much exercise. Aerobics expert Dr. Kenneth Cooper has found that running more than 25 miles a week can cause muscle and joint injuries.

What is important to remember about any exercise program is that it should be enjoyable and fit into your lifestyle. A balanced approach that offers a variety of activities seems to be the best.

The two ways of measuring your need for exercise are looking at heart rate and oxygen consumption. Obviously, it is easier to measure heart rate. To take your heart rate, find your pulse at the wrist or neck, and count for ten seconds. Then multiply it by six. A simpler way to determine if your exercise is sufficient is to notice if your pulse rate, breathing, and respiration increase during or after your workout (they should). Exercise experts have worked out what they consider to be optimum heart rates during and after exercise. If you are interested, you may look further into this.

LESSON 7

Purpose: To teach the children about the benefits of exercise.

Materials Needed

Tape II, Side 2, Dialogue 7

Workbook Activity 7-1

Directions

1. Discuss the benefits of exercise using the "Background for the Teacher" section and emphasize the following points:

Exercise is good for you

Exercises are needed to keep the body working properly

The heart and lungs need exercise to function at their peak

Exercise aids in the growth and development of muscle patterns, strength, and flexibility

Muscles feel better when they are worked

Exercise improves emotional stability and alertness

Exercise improves the body's ability to combat the negative effects of stress

2. Talk about the components of exercise. Use the background material to define the terms "strength," "muscle endurance," "flexibility," and "cardiovascular endurance." You may use the following brief outline if you do not want to go into too much detail:

　　a. *Strength.* This is the amount of force you can exert, that is, how much you can lift. Sit-ups, push-ups, and weight training build strength.

　　b. *Muscle endurance.* This is how long you can hold or keep up strength. You build muscle endurance by repeated activities, such as running, jumping rope, and cycling.

　　c. *Flexibility.* This is a measure of the degree of motion in joints, muscles, tendons, and ligaments. Yoga and stretching exercises can increase flexibility.

　　d. *Heart or cardiovascular endurance.* Sustained activity that works the heart and lungs helps develop endurance. This is perhaps the most important element in physical fitness. It is also referred to as aerobic exercise. You need 30 minutes of this three to four times a week. Swimming, running, and cycling are good exercises for developing heart endurance.

3. Ask the students what kinds of exercise they get. Do they get enough aerobic exercise?

4. Teach the students how to take their pulse and ask them to fill in the chart in their workbooks. (See Activity 7-1.)

5. Play Tape II, Side 2, Dialogue 7. (The dialogue follows this lesson.) No heavy exercise is done on this tape, of course, because it would not be appropriate in this setting. This tape applies movement awareness techniques to exercise in order to get spinal flexibility. It then goes on to more traditional stretching and movement. Before you begin the tape, look at the illustrations accompanying the dialogue so that you can explain the movements should the children have difficulty.

Follow-up Suggestions:

1. Using Activity 7-1 in the workbook, have the children keep a record of the amount of aerobic exercise they do each week.

2. Four weeks later, have the children repeat the workbook exercise on pulse rate to see if their pulse rate has improved.

TAPE II, SIDE 2, DIALOGUE 7

I'd like you to sit near the front of your chair, feet on the floor, arms at your sides. You are going to be moving your spine in several directions. You will be moving it like a chain, link by link.

Would you please put your hand on the base of your neck in back and find the biggest bump there. That is your seventh cervical vertebra. Move down and feel the next bone or vertebra. Keep going and feel the parts of your spine, one by one, as far as you can reach. Now take your hand away. We will not use the hands anymore. Put them comfortably in your lap. We will try to move each of the vertebrae separately. I'd like you to close your eyes. This blocks out outside interference and makes it easier to pay attention to how your body feels.

Start by bringing your head forward, chin towards chest, until you can sense the feel of the seventh vertebra. Remember, you just found it with your hand. Now you're trying to just notice it. Come back up. The next time you go down, you will try to sense, or feel, that same bone and the next one down, which is called the first thoracic. Go down and come up. Now go down to these two plus the next vertebra. Come up.

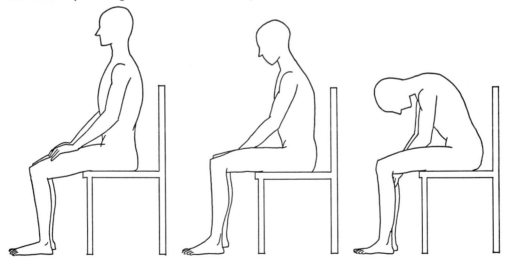

Tape II, Side 2, Dialogue 7, continued

What we're trying to teach you is to be able to feel and move each separate vertebra. You may not be able to feel each one separately if this is one of the first times you are hearing this tape. You will get better each time you practice it.

We're going to move the body, vertebra by vertebra, in all the directions that the spine will go—forward, to both sides, and to the back. Listen to the directions and do not start until told to do so. You will start with the head moving forward, then to the right, then to the left, and then to the back. Each time you complete going through all four directions, you will try to move down one vertebra so that you've added one more. So, we'll be starting with the seventh cervical and going through all four directions. Then it will be the seventh cervical and the next one and the one after that. Notice all of the vertebrae each time. We will keep moving down until we include the seventh cervical and the next five vertebrae in our movements in all directions.

Ready now. Begin by moving your head forward until you feel the seventh cervical vertebra, and now come back up. Now move your head to the right until you feel that same vertebra, and come back up. Now to the left...and up...and back...and up...Again, go forward and feel the seventh cervical bend and the next one too. Now come up...Go to the right now...Feel the same two...and up...the left now...and up...and back...and up. Okay. We're going to try to feel the seventh cervical and the next two this time. Bend the head forward. You'll be going farther this time. Feel all three and come up. Now to the right side...and up...the left...and up...and back...and up. Can you feel each vertebra as you move? Let's add three more, all at once, so we move six separately. Do this at your own speed—go forward, right, left, back, and up.

Now you're going to go forward, moving each vertebra separately, going as far down as you can go, and then coming back up, feeling each vertebra as you move. When you go down you should be able to touch your head to your knee. Go at your own speed in all four directions now.

Now we are going to move our lower spine. Sit tall in your chair and feel your spine. It should be straight and lifted. I want you to slump in your chair by letting your spine relax. It will get rounded. Okay, now sit tall again. We will do that again. This time, notice the movement of your spine when you collapse. Go ahead and slump. Now sit up again. When you collapse, make the movement down and up by rolling the spine, starting in the tailbone (the bottom of your spine). The tailbone and lower spine connect to your pelvis and the whole structure can move in many directions.

This time when you move, I would like you to curl your tailbone down (like you did when you collapsed), but don't let the upper body sink. Feel the bones as you move. Do it. You can put your hand on the small of your back. As you curl, that part will move towards the back of your chair. That's good.

You can move in the opposite direction and make an arch. Instead of rounding downwards, curve and make an arch. To do this, you move so that your stomach moves forward, away from the back of your chair. Go ahead. Now move back to center. If you go from curling to arching, you get a rocking motion.

Tape II, Side 2, Dialogue 7, continued

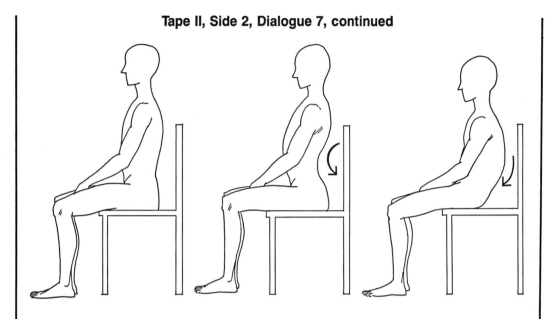

Try this movement now: go back to the resting position and try it one more time. Now I want you to practice going from the curl, going back to center, going forward into the arch, and back to center. This will seem like a rocking motion. We're going to do this same rocking motion with the head included also. So let's do it with the head alone now. Try it...head forward...and up...back...don't strain on the backward motion...and up. Now try to coordinate all of these motions. As you curl, you let your head drop towards your chest and as you arch, your head goes backwards. Try it all together. Begin with the tailbone curl and head forward and then move through to the other motion. Ready. Go...curl...and head forward...roll back to center...arch...head back...and back to center. Again.

Now we're trying a sideways motion. Do this with me right now. Lift one hip up slightly and now let it drop again. Do the same with the other hip, and again. Now try to do this smoothly from one to the other so that you are rocking from side to side. Now, since you're all so good at this, we'll add the head. As you rock side to side, move the head toward the hip that is lifted. If you lift the hip up on the left, move your head towards the left shoulder and, of course, do the opposite as you rock to the other side. When you rock, be sure that you lift the hip to make yourself rock, not that you lean and the hip just happens to come along. Try it. Rock with left hip up to the right...left...right...left. Be sure you take the head with you.

We're going to combine everything now. Now let's review all the directions slowly with the head, hips, and tailbone together. Curl forward with your tailbone and head...go to the right with your hip and head...to the back with the tailbone and head...to the left with hip and head...and back to center. We've just gone four directions with our head

Tape II, Side 2, Dialogue 7, continued

and with our pelvis. If you move slowly in all directions, you can make circles. Think of trying to make smooth circles. Practice going clockwise and counterclockwise. Let's go together forward, right side, back, left side, center. Reverse—forward, left side, back, right side, center. And one more time now on your own.

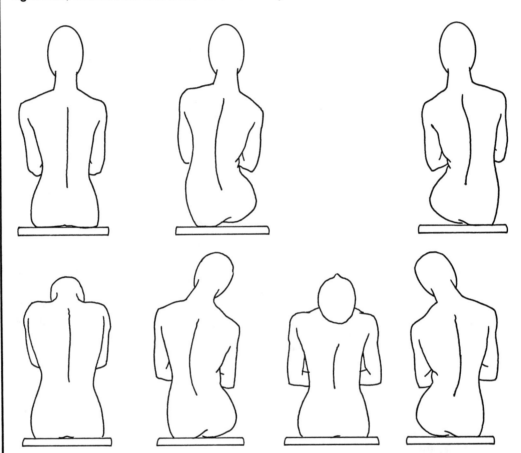

It's time to stand up now. Just stand with your feet slightly apart, toes pointed straight ahead. Stretch both arms over your head and keep them there. Reach your right arm even higher, so that the whole right side gets pulled with it. Keep your arm up but let the shoulder drop. Now reach with the left arm and drop the shoulder. Right again, and left. Drop your arms down to your sides and shrug your shoulders up to your ears. Now drop them down again...and up...and down...Good. Stretch your arms overhead again and let's repeat that. Stretch right...left...right...left. Drop your arms...shrug your shoulders...up and down and up and down. Good. Now circle both shoulders forward...up...back...down. Now reverse that—back...up...forward...and down. One more time.

Now let's just bounce the body. Bend at the knees. Let the arms hang loosely and bounce loosely like a rag doll. Your whole body will probably shake. Now let your upper body fall forward as you bounce and then come back up. Now arch backwards and come up again, still bouncing. Now take your upper body to the right; and back up; and drop

Tape II, Side 2, Dialogue 7, continued

left and back up. Keep bouncing. Can you make a circle with your torso in those directions while you bounce? Forward...side...back...side...forward. Good. Go the other way.

We're going to work our feet now. Would you bring the heel of your right foot up until the toes bend, and then pick the toes up off the floor and point them towards the floor? You will really have to work the foot. Now put the toes back on the floor, but not with the heel all the way down. Dancers call this *demi-pointe.* Then go back to flat. We will do that four times. Do it with me. Halfway up...point...halfway down...down...halfway up...point...half down...down. Now we'll do that in one smooth motion, but don't leave out any part. Really work the whole foot. Feel the bones...one...two...three...four.

Now let's do the left foot. Stretch to half-point, push off, and point, back to half, and down. Four times with me—one, two, three, four. One, two, three four. Halfway, point, halfway down, one, two, three, four. Now move the whole foot and do this smoothly four times—one, two, three, four.

Good. Now let's run in place. We'll start gently, arms loose, shoulders relaxed, feet hardly off the floor. Go at your own speed. Now pick up your feet a little more. Are you getting tired? Try to keep going. Be relaxed, though. Breathe as you move. Go at your own pace and build up speed. When you get tired, slowly decrease speed. Keep decreasing until you are almost moving in slow motion. Slowly sit down and relax. Do your slow, deep breathing for the next minute. Begin. Stay calm, stay loose, and stay relaxed.

Name _____

Date _____

Aerobic Exercise Record

Resting pulse _____

Running in place for _____ minutes

Pulse after running _____

Pulse five minutes later _____

Pulse each minute after (if not back to resting pulse yet) _____ _____ _____ _____ _____

    Name each kind of exercise that you do in one week, and include the amount of time you spend doing it. Mark all aerobic exercises with an *A*.

Date	Exercise	How Long I Spent at It

LESSON 8

Final Relaxation Sequence

BACKGROUND FOR THE TEACHER

This is a completely taped lesson. The tape takes the students on a trip to idyllic Hawaii by way of their imaginations. This final relaxation sequence uses all of the techniques taught in the previous tapes: breathing, muscle relaxation, imagery, movement awareness, movement exercises, and complete body relaxation.

LESSON 8

Purpose: To have the children use all of the previously learned techniques in order to become totally relaxed.

Materials Needed

Tape II, Side 2, Dialogue 8

Directions

Play Tape II, Side 2, Dialogue 8 as a final relaxation lesson.

TAPE II, SIDE 2, DIALOGUE 8

For our last tape, since you've all been so good and have been learning your relaxation skills so well, you're being rewarded with the trip of a lifetime. We're all going to Hawaii on this tape. I hope you really get to go there some day, but for now, I hope this final tape will help you relax as much as a trip to Hawaii really would.

I want you to close your eyes and sit back comfortably, and try to really use your imagination and picture everything that is suggested. We'll start our trip on a giant 747 airplane. Sit down in your seat. You've got lots of room. Get comfortable. Scan your body. Does it feel tight anywhere? You know how to tense and relax parts of your body. You can do this to any part that feels tight or, even better, just release the tension there without tensing it first. When you think you've relaxed every tense part, scan your body again and see if there is still tension anywhere. If there is, release it there too. Now that you're relaxed, we'll continue on the trip. Remember to keep your eyes closed for the whole trip. Even if I say to look at something, do the looking with your eyes closed. You already know how you can see with your mind. Take a few long, slow, deep breaths and relax. Look out the window and see how blue the sky is and see the bright sun. Remember, your eyes are closed. You are even closer to it in this plane, and you feel it even warmer than you would down on the ground. Watch the soft, white clouds float by. Imagine yourself out there in the clouds—floating and drifting, with the warm sun on you. All right now. This was a fast plane. We're getting very close to Hawaii. As we start to land, let's get even more relaxed. We're at 30,000 feet now and starting our descent. As we get closer to the ground, let's get more and more relaxed. You are relaxed now, but we're slowly drifting down to 20,000 feet, and as you watch the clouds drift by, try to feel a little more relaxed than you did at 30,000 feet when we began to descend. Even if it's just a tiny bit more relaxed, that's fine. Try to feel it. Now breathe deeply as we slowly go down to 10,000 feet. Relax a little more. We're going from 10,000 feet slowly to the ground now. Feel a little more relaxed as we drift down to a perfect landing.

All right, we're here. Keep your eyes closed now and imagine what Hawaii looks like. We're leaving the airport and cruising in a beautiful convertible, just relaxing and watching the scenery go by. There is a perfect blue sky and a bright, warm sun. We see palm trees and smiling people as we head towards the beach. Overhead is a hang glider just floating in the breeze, like a giant bird. We arrive at the beach and can't wait to get down to the waterfront. Picture yourself walking over the sand now. You've got on your bathing suit, of course. Feel the texture of the sand. It is soft and gives under your feet. It

Tape II, Side 2, Dialogue 8. continued

is warm, but not hot. Picture the water in front of you. It's a brilliant blue color, with patches of green. The sky is perfectly clear and blue and the sun is so nice and warm. The waves move slowly across the water and there is just enough breeze to keep you comfortable and to make the leaves of the palm trees sway slowly. Smell the fresh, salt air. Find a comfortable spot on the beach and sit down. Don't lie down yet. While you're seated you're going to do some relaxing exercises. Do these now, don't just imagine them. Roll your head back and to the right, to the front, to the left and back to center. Let's loosen up those neck muscles. One more time, by yourself. Now two times the other way. Good. Extend your arms all the way up in the air and reach your head up too. Now let them slowly come back down. Stretch your right arm to the side. Do it slowly so you don't hit the person next to you. Start at the shoulder joint as you stretch. Let it feel like electricity moving through your shoulder, down your arm, into your hand and then out through your fingers. There should only be a little tension as you stretch out your arms. Don't hold them very tight. Now release your hand, arm, elbow, and shoulder and we'll go to the left arm. Slowly stretch it out to the side, starting the movement at the shoulder. Feel that electricity going down the whole arm. Now release that arm. Let it hang. Take a deep breath. Smell that salty, fresh Hawaiian air. Now do both arms together. Slowly. Don't hit anyone. Out to the side. Send that low tension electricity down from the shoulders and out the fingers...and relax them. Do the same with your legs now. Stretch the right leg out in front of you in the aisle. Send the electricity down the thigh, past the knee, to the calf, the feet and out the toes. Now release. Stretch out the left leg. Send the electricity down through it, out the toes, and release. Once more with both at once. Send that electricity down, and out, and release. Now, like a rubber band stretching out but never getting taut, stretch anywhere you need it. Let your body guide your stretching and not your mind. All right, go ahead. Then relax.

Let's really relax into our beach scene. Keep your eyes closed. Take a deep breath of air, smell the sea. Feel the freshness. Let's breathe in some good, long breaths. I'll count it out for you. Breathe in now, 1, 2, 3, 4, 5, 6. Hold it. Exhale 2, 3, 4, 5, 6, 7, 8. Again. In 2, 3, 4, 5, 6. Hold 2, 3, 4. Out 2, 3, 4, 5, 6, 7, 8. Now let's exhale with a hiss. Make it sound like the wind going through the palm trees. Okay, in, out—hisssss. In, out—hisssss.

All right. You're still on the beach, lying in the sand. Really feel that sun now. Feel the warmth on your hands. That Hawaiian sun is warm and soothing. There is a slight breeze so that you are not uncomfortable. As a matter of fact, as you feel your hands warming, notice a cool breeze across your forehead. Think about the warmth again. Think about how nice and warm your hands and feet and arms are. Feel the sun on you. Feel the sun warming you and warming up your insides.

Let's leave our spot on the sand now. Imagine yourself out on the water now, on a raft. It's one of those really comfortable ones with a raised pillow. You're floating on the water, just drifting. It's safe, of course, since there's a reef to prevent you from drifting too far out. Breathe in deeply a few times. Feel the sun's warm rays on you as you slowly drift across the water. Picture yourself looking from your spot on the raft over to the shore. Imagine the most beautiful Hawaiian beach. The palm trees have leaves swaying in the breeze. Smile inside of you as you feel content. Look on the beach and you will see your private relaxation helper, the one you used on our other tape. Smile to this person. Float in towards the shore and greet this person. As you get off the raft, reach out your hand and take the hand of your person and walk off down the beach. Smile inside again

Tape II, Side 2, Dialogue 8, continued

because you know that you will learn even more about how to relax now and how to stay calm and happy. As you watch yourself walk off with your relaxation helper, you can end your trip and slowly open your eyes, loosen any tight areas, and slowly stretch anything that needs stretching. Congratulations. You are a relaxation graduate. But don't stop here. The more you listen to your tapes and practice, the better you'll get at it, the calmer you will be able to stay, and the happier you can be.

LESSON 9

The Physical and Behavioral Signs of Stress

BACKGROUND FOR THE TEACHER

Children react to stress in many ways. As we have mentioned, stress manifests itself in chronic muscle tension. The result is poor use of the body and a limited range of motion. Children may also develop stress-induced illnesses or symptoms. Headaches, stomach aches and other gastrointestinal problems, allergies, and tics and other mannerisms may develop. Children may begin showing signs of so-called type-A behavior, whereby they become fast paced, rushed, and nervous. (See Lesson 18.) Hyperactivity may result, and children may withdraw. Some may become loners in or out of school or in both environments. School phobias develop in some. Others may simply withdraw from the stressful aspects of school. That is, they may not withdraw from the physical school situation or from contact with other children, but may not participate in class, may not answer in class, and may not do their homework or classwork. Some may simply turn off; apathy and listlessness may result. School burnout is a new term for an old problem. Premature structuring is a possible reaction to stress. This occurs when a child may choose one thing and concentrate on that at

77

the expense of everything else. These children devote all their time to something at which they can succeed and eliminate the stress or possibility of stress in areas in which they may fail. Some children try to escape stress by using alcohol or drugs. Some escape by embracing cults that promise a secure "family" and a caring environment, free from pressure or the need to think for themselves. The alarming number of suicides in young people attests to the fact that some seek a permanent release from the stresses of life.

It may be a long time before stress overloads a person's system enough that a symptom develops, so lack of a symptom does not necessarily mean that the person is not suffering from stress. On the other hand, if a person does have some of these symptoms, it may be a sign that he or she is feeling the effects of stress. Everybody needs to relax, but when symptoms of stress appear, it is even more important. This lesson includes a list of symptoms that can be caused by stress. Realize that other things can cause them too. Also, remember that even healthy people may have some of these symptoms once in a while or for a short period. If many of them occur or if they stay for a long time, there is most likely a problem.

LESSON 9

Purpose: To show the children how people react to stress, both physiologically and behaviorally, in order to recognize their own signs of stress; and to show the children how prevalent stress-induced problems are.

Materials Needed

Workbook Activity 9-1

Directions

1. Ask the children how many of them have had a headache or stomach ache in the past day or week. Ask how many know someone at home who had one in the past day or week. Next, ask the children how they feel and how they act when they are feeling stressed. Ask them what happens to their body when they get upset. You will probably hear about breathing changes, muscle tightening, stomach changes (aching, nausea, diarrhea), cold hands, sweating, jaw clenching, shaking hands, tics or twitches, dizziness, heart speeding, and headaches.

2. Discuss material from the background section so that the children can see how they and others may react to stress.

3. Next, have the students use the checklist in the workbook (see Activity 9-1). Ask them to check off in the "me" section those symptoms they experience rarely (less than once a week) in the "R" column and the ones they experience often in the "O" column. Then have them fill in the "my relative" section for an adult they know well. Let them see if there is a big difference.

4. When the checklists are completed, make a class tally sheet so that the students can see how prevalent the symptoms are even in this small group. Show the number of adults with the symptoms and the number of children with the symptoms. Explain that the adult list may be understated because they don't really know all of the symptoms that the relative has.

Follow-up Suggestions

1. Have the children add to the list (in a different color pen) each time they experience a symptom. Let them see if doing their relaxation exercises has cut down on any symptoms by comparing the frequency before and after learning the exercises. The children should know that, as soon as they begin to experience any symptom, they should do a relaxation exercise. (Depending on how far you have gotten with the tapes, they may have a few or many techniques to try.)

2. If you have not discussed it already, you might talk now about non-physical behaviors that children may exhibit, including dropping out, withdrawing, becoming a loner; premature structuring (devoting all one's energy to one endeavor, such as basketball, piano, or coin collecting); cults; suicide; and drugs or alcohol. For more information on drug abuse, contact:

National Clearinghouse for Drug Abuse Information
P.O. Box 416
Kensington, Maryland 20795
301-443-6500
(allow three to four weeks for publications)

National Institute for Drug Abuse—Prevention Unit
1-800-638-2045
(curriculum information and planning)

Signs of Stress

DIRECTIONS: Look at the following symptoms of stress. Place a checkmark in the column marked "R" if you experience this symptom rarely. Place a checkmark in the column marked "O" if you experience it often. Fill in the symptoms for a relative, too.

Me R	Me O		My Relative R	My Relative O
		1. Headaches		
		2. Stomach problems—diarrhea, constipation, nausea, heartburn, urinating often		
		3. High blood pressure or heart pounding		
		4. Pain in neck, lower back, shoulders, jaw		
		5. Muscle jerks or tics		
		6. Eating problems—no appetite, constant eating, full feeling without eating		
		7. Sleeping problems—unable to fall asleep, wake up in middle of the night, nightmares		
		8. Fainting		
		9. General feeling of tiredness		
		10. Shortness of breath		
		11. Dry throat or mouth		
		12. Unable to sit still—extra energy		
		13. Teeth grinding		
		14. Stuttering		
		15. Uncontrollable crying or not being able to cry		
		16. Smoking		
		17. Use excessive alcohol		
		18. Use drugs		
		19. Increased use of medication—aspirin, tranquilizers, etc.		
		20. General anxiety, nervous feelings, or tenseness		
		21. Dizziness and weakness		
		22. Irritable and easily set off		
		23. Depressed		

Me			My Relative	
R	O		R	O
		24. Accident prone		
		25. Feeling angry in general		
		26. Feeling overwhelmed and unable to cope—want to run away, cry, or end it all		
		27. Doing weird things without thinking		
		28. Nervous laughter, easily startled, jumpy		
		29. Always concerned about disease and death		
		30. Bored with life		
		31. Always worried about money		
		32. Afraid of weekends or vacations		
		33. Feeling that you can't discuss problems with anyone else		
		34. Afraid of heights or closed spaces		
		35. Feeling rejected all the time, especially by your family		
		36. Unable to concentrate or finish things you start		
		37. Never laugh		
		38. Allergies		
		39. Always in a hurry		
		40. Don't have friends and may not care about being with other people		
		41. Don't do your assignments		
		42. Can do one thing well and most of your time is spent on it		
		43. Joining a cult group		

LESSON 10

The Relaxation Response and a Short Super-Relaxation Sequence

BACKGROUND FOR THE TEACHER

The term "relaxation response" has been popularized by Herbert Benson and Miriam Z. Klipper in their book *The Relaxation Response* (New York: Avon, 1976). Dr. Benson studied people meditating and found that the following changes occurred in their bodies:

- Breathing changes (less oxygen taken in, less carbon dioxide exhaled, and slowed breathing rate)
- Changes in sweating (decreased sweating from the palms and soles)

- Blood changes (less cholesterol and lactate and less blood flow to the skeletal muscles)
- Muscle changes (less activity)
- Brain wave changes (alpha and theta waves increased)

Basically, Dr. Benson found that when a person meditates he or she experiences the opposite of what occurs in a stress reaction, that is, muscle and sympathetic nervous system activity are decreased. This pattern of changes is termed the relaxation response. The individual did not have to try to change each thing, but simply had to relax.

The meditation technique studied has several components that are similar to the relaxation techniques described in this lesson. The person stops doing other activities, moves to a quiet spot, closes his or her eyes, and switches thoughts from the usual large number of thoughts (many of which have emotional content) to a few or only one. Many of these meditative techniques have people think of one word, and have them return to this thought when other thoughts intrude.

By using these relaxation techniques, we can achieve the same type of physiological changes and the same pattern of relaxation that occur in the relaxation response. Once the techniques have been learned, it should not be necessary to do a tape every time a person needs to relax. The student should be able to recognize the feeling of relaxation that he or she has achieved through these exercises, and should be able to reproduce that feeling quickly.

This is very important because you want the children to be able to take a very short relaxation break many times each day, such as

- Before a potentially stressful situation (such as before giving a report in front of the class)
- During a stressful situation (such as while being reprimanded or during a test)
- After a stressful situation (such as after having been reprimanded)

These situations may occur five, ten, twenty, or even fifty times in a day. With practice the children will eventually be so adept at relaxing that they will be able to make major changes in their body's stress reaction during a very short relaxation break.

It can help to have signs or symbols displayed around the room to remind the children to relax. Display posters or little "R's" around the room, anything to jog their memories and remind them to relax when they feel stress.

LESSON 10

Purpose: To show the children how to use their knowledge of the feeling of relaxation to shorten the time needed to relax.

Materials Needed

None

Directions

1. Briefly explain the material from the background section. Explain that it is advisable to take one long relaxation break each day. It should be at least as long as one of the tapes (15 to 20 minutes). Many people find the evening to be the time that they have that long a period available, but a relaxation break can be taken any time—on a train ride, after school, or any time at all. Be sure to reinforce the idea that there are many times in the day that they face stressful situations and that their bodies will react with a stress response.

Point out to the students that they now know what it feels like to be relaxed. They have learned how to release muscle tension, warm their hands (which slows down their stress-type nervous system activity), and think calming thoughts.

2. Explain that you will be going over a short super-relaxation sequence that combines a few of the techniques they already know. Explain the sequence that follows and practice it with the students:

- Close your eyes and try to stop thinking about anything. You may even say to yourself in your head, "Stop thinking."
- Take two or three long deep breaths, just as you did on the breathing tape. For the rest of the two minutes, keep breathing deeply.
- Do two slow head rolls and two shoulder rolls. (Head roll: move your head down to your chest, to one shoulder, slightly to the back behind you, to the other shoulder, and back up. Shoulder roll: make circles forward and backward with your shoulders.)
- Scan your body for any tight muscles. Concentrate on releasing those muscles.
- Concentrate on your hands; think about warming them.
- Get a pleasant thought in your mind. (You might think about your perfect place.) Smile inside to yourself.
- *If you are feeling calm,* say to yourself, "I am calm and relaxed."
- Take two slow, deep breaths.
- Slowly open your eyes. Feel calm and alert.

This process should only take one to two minutes. An important point is the phrase "I am calm and relaxed." On the relaxing phrases tape, the child was told to repeat phrases such as, "my right arm is heavy" or "my left leg is warm." The purpose was to help the child begin to concentrate on these kinds of feelings and to be able to produce them eventually. The phrase, "I am calm and relaxed" is to be used only when the child is actually feeling that way. By pairing this phrase with the feeling, the child should be able to more easily reproduce the feeling simply by repeating the phrase to himself or herself. This can allow for a rapid relaxation simply by repeating that phrase and trying to "feel" the "relaxation response." Therefore, until the child gets really good at relaxing, this phrase will be used only when the feeling is actually being experienced. Later on, it will be able to be used to help trigger the relaxation.

Follow-up Suggestion

Be sure to allow as many two-minute super-relaxation breaks during the day as possible so that the children can practice and so that the benefits of relaxing and slowing down during the day can be felt by them. You will feel the benefits, too, in the little improvements that the students begin exhibiting.

LESSON 11

Time as a Stressor

BACKGROUND FOR THE TEA[CHER]

Time pressures are a very prevalent source of s[tress. Some] pressures cannot be avoided, such as homework assignments[, writing r]eports, and studying for tests. Let the students know that they [can av]oid some of the pressures through a course of direct action. Fo[r example,] of the stress brought about by a report's being due can be ease[d by starting] it early and researching it well. The deadline is there, but the[y don't] have to worry about finishing in time or whether they are doi[ng well. In] the course of everyday life, there are many tasks, chores, and re[sponsibilitie]s that must be taken care of. Many children get themselves in trouble simply because of poor planning and time management. They feel pressured to get things done and may feel that they simply don't have enough time. Most children can learn that with proper budgeting of time, things can be accomplished more efficiently and that they can rid themselves of some of the stress and worry.

LESSON 11

Purpose: To show the children how to set priorities, budget time, and make a schedule.

Materials Needed

Workbook Activities 11-1, 11-2, and 11-3

Directions

1. Make a list of all the activities that you, the teacher, expect to get done in class in one day (or this class period, if departmentalized) with the students. If this does not seem as if it is a lot of things to do, include everything that you plan to accomplish all day, both in and out of school. Ask the children if it seems as if all of it can be done. Let them help you set up a time schedule for doing everything.

2. Have the children complete Activity 11-1 in their workbooks. The list of "Things to Do" should include only those obligations that have a deadline today. The other lists are to be filled in with definite commitments, such as tests to take, dental appointments to meet, parties to attend, and so on.

3. Then have the children list the things that they would like to get done on Activity 11-2. Going to a ball game, shopping for clothes, visiting friends, and so on may be included on this sheet.

4. Use this exercise as a springboard to a discussion of setting priorities and budgeting time. The children should realize that they often spend much time and emotional energy worrying about things that cannot be dealt with yet. They also can see that although there are many things that they would like to get done, there are very few that *must* be done immediately. A point that you want to be sure to get across is that by setting down on paper (or at least making a mental note of) the things to be done and when, the students can see what time is available for other activities they would like to do. This makes it easier to prepare for obligations and helps to prevent their worrying about things at times when it accomplishes nothing constructive. Making schedules and lists of commitments can also help children to see where their free time lies so that they can use it well.

5. Further demonstrate how to schedule their time by copying the "Scheduling My Day" chart (see Activity 11-2) onto the chalkboard and filling it in with *your* commitments and leisure activities for the day. Distinguish (with different colors, for example) between real commitments (such as your hours teaching, going to graduate school, taking tennis lessons) and desired activities that you will do if there is time (such as watching a certain television program, visiting a friend, or reading a book). Show the children that there are usually gaps in even the busiest schedules where activities of choice can be enjoyed.

6. Have the children fill in their own "Scheduling My Day" charts in their workbooks. The things that *must* be done can be in one color and things that they would like to do can be in another color.

Follow-up Suggestions

1. Have the children check off things from their schedule as they are completed. When certain things are not done after several days or even weeks, the children may see that they were not so important after all, or that they had problems as a result of not doing them.

2. Have the children complete their goal sheets in the workbook (see Activity 11-3). Go over this activity with them.

Things to Do

DIRECTIONS: Make a list of everything you *must* do in the left column, and everything you would *like* to do in the right column.

	Things I Must Do	Things I Would Like to Do
Today		
Tomorrow		
This Week		
This Month		

Name _____

Date _____

Scheduling My Day

DIRECTIONS: Use one color to write in things you *must* do in each time period. Use another color to write in those things you would *like* to do in each period.

8–9 A.M.						
9–10						
10–11						
11–12 P.M.						
12–1						
1–2						
2–3						
3–4						
4–5						
5–6						
6–7						
7–8						
8–9						
9–10						
10–11						
11–12						
after 12						

My Goals

DIRECTIONS: Complete the following sentences.

My lifetime goals are _____

_____

_____

_____

_____

_____

I want to spend the next three years _____

_____

_____

_____

_____

_____

_____

If I had only six more months to live _____

_____

_____

_____

_____

_____

_____

LESSON 12

Knowing Your Limits

BACKGROUND FOR THE TEACHER

Helping children to realize just how much they can handle prevents them from exceeding their limits and causing stress due to the overload and frustration. This goes along with the skill of learning to say no in Lesson 13.

The children will also learn where there is room for improving their present capabilities, a necessary skill if they are to grow and mature.

LESSON 12

Purpose: To let the children see that each of them has different capabilities in different areas.

Materials Needed

Workbook Activities 12-1, 12-2, 12-3, and 12-4

Directions

1. Ask two children to do the following multiplication problem on the chalkboard or on chart paper. (If they are at a low skill level and are unable to do this problem, give them instead a difficult problem that is within their capabilities.)

$$
\begin{array}{r}
45628 \\
\times\ 23587 \\
\hline
\end{array}
$$

As the two students are trying to do the problem, keep flashing a different number of fingers raised and, each time you do, ask the two students to call out how many fingers are raised. This will prove very distracting for many and will prevent them from completing the problem. If they are able to do both at once, you can also ask them to call out the name of each child in the class as they are doing the problem. The point is that it is difficult to do several things at once, and it is possible to be overloaded beyond your limits.

2. To show that each of us has different capabilities for different tasks, have the children turn to Activity 12-1 in their workbooks. Read each series of numbers aloud after instructing the class to memorize each series and be prepared to write each one in the spaces provided. After reading each series, have the children wait 10 to 15 seconds and then write the series.

Now read each of the following series:

4,8,7,9
2,8,0,6,5
9,6,3,2,8,7
6,0,8,5,7,6,1
9,0,1,7,8,5,4,2
8,1,7,0,9,6,9,4,2
9,7,5,7,0,1,3,8,3,7
9,6,4,0,1,7,3,5,6,4,8
9,8,0,1,6,4,7,2,1,4,0,5
8,1,9,4,0,3,5,3,2,9,0,8,6
6,9,8,4,3,0,5,3,1,7,6,5,2,9
8,4,9,1,0,6,3,7,2,9,6,1,5,4,0

3. Ask the children to turn to Activity 12-2 in the workbook. Tell them that the purpose of this activity is to show them how many words per minute they can read with what degree of comprehension. Time the reading of the story; you will

need a watch with a second hand. As each child raises his or her hand, tell him or her the time it took to finish reading and have the child record it in the work book. Upon completion of reading and recording the time, have each child cover the story and answer the questions that follow (without referring to the story). Later, help each child figure out his or her reading speed by dividing the number of words (570) by the number of minutes it took to finish the story. For example, John takes one minute and 40 seconds to finish. Divide 570 words by $1\frac{2}{3}$ minutes ($570 \div \frac{5}{3} = 570 \times \frac{3}{5}$) to get 342 words per minute. Then, go over the answers to the comprehension questions and give each child a comprehension score.

As it is unlikely that any two will have the exact same speed and comprehension, this exercise will illustrate that they each have a different capacity. Be sure the children realize that they must learn what their capacities are for speed and workload and try not to overload themselves. This applies to all situations, not just to school subjects. You, the teacher, may also begin to see that you need to allow some leeway for this when you decide on the workload for individual students or the class, and when you have class lessons geared to a certain speed and load capacity.

4. The students should now be starting to realize that each of them has a maximum capacity at any given time to do only so much in a certain area. Make the point that there is a limit to the number of responsibilities and tasks they can handle and how much stress they can take. This limit fluctuates, but students should be aware of what their capacity is so they don't try to exceed it.

Talk a little bit about competitiveness and always trying to do what everybody else is doing. Students need to know that they have to do what is right for themselves.

5. Have the children fill in the chart in Activity 12-3 in the workbook. You can make a class sheet to show how each of them has chosen different loads that they feel they could handle in different situations. The students can also begin to see that in some areas they are not doing anything approaching the limits of what they could handle.

Follow-up Suggestion

Over the next few days have the children complete Activity 12-4 in the workbook. Go over these charts with the students and discuss the reasons things do not get completed.

Answers to Activity 12-2

1. 1943
2. Jacques Cousteau
3. fish, sponges, coral, moray eels, lobster, octopus, manta rays, barracuda, sharks
4. to buy or rent the equipment
5. sponges
6. moray eels
7. manta rays

What Are Your Limits?

DIRECTIONS: Listen carefully as your teacher reads a series of numbers, one set at a time. When your teacher has finished one series, write the numbers—in the same order—on the spaces provided here. Remember, one series will be done at a time.

___ ___ ___ ___

___ ___ ___ ___ ___

___ ___ ___ ___ ___ ___

___ ___ ___ ___ ___ ___ ___

___ ___ ___ ___ ___ ___ ___ ___

___ ___ ___ ___ ___ ___ ___ ___ ___

___ ___ ___ ___ ___ ___ ___ ___ ___

___ ___ ___ ___ ___ ___ ___ ___ ___ ___

___ ___ ___ ___ ___ ___ ___ ___ ___ ___ ___

___ ___ ___ ___ ___ ___ ___ ___ ___ ___ ___ ___

___ ___ ___ ___ ___ ___ ___ ___ ___ ___ ___ ___ ___

___ ___ ___ ___ ___ ___ ___ ___ ___ ___ ___ ___ ___

Reading and Comprehension

Read the following story and answer the questions that follow it. Do not begin to read until your teacher tells you to. Raise your hand when you have finished reading. Your teacher will tell you how long it took you, and you will write down the time.

Scuba Diving

Scuba diving is getting to be more and more popular each year. Today there are thousands and thousands of people who are donning their air tanks, putting on flippers, and diving under the water to mingle with the fish and coral. It is hard to believe that not many years ago, the number of people to ever have seen that unbelievable world beneath the surface probably numbered no more than a few hundred.

Until 1943, when Jacques Cousteau (the same man you see on television programs) invented *scuba* (*s*elf-contained *u*nderwater *b*reathing *a*pparatus) gear, hardly anyone was able to dive except for those wearing the heavy metal equipment that was attached by hoses to a boat above it. These suits were the kind you might have seen or read about in *20,000 Leagues Under the Sea*. They had heavy helmets and made you look like a robot. Cousteau's invention made it possible to strap a tank of air right onto your back. You didn't have to be attached to the boat at all. This made scuba diving much easier and much less expensive as well. As a result, many more people began to visit the amazing world beneath the sea.

If you ever get a chance to try scuba diving you will see why so many people are taking up this sport. Once you get below the surface of the water, you are in another world. You are the outsider, and the tank on your back is your reminder of that. If you choose a good spot you might find yourself swimming in the most gorgeous jungle of coral that you can imagine, with giant sponges and thousands of unbelievably beautiful fish all around.

You will see every color of the rainbow in the fish that swim in this coral jungle. If you look closely you will see even more life in the coral and in the holes and under rocks. Moray eels can be seen peeking out of their holes. They look very fierce with their mouths open showing their sharp teeth. They will not come out of their holes to hurt you, so just don't reach in with your hands to places that you can't see. Tiny shrimp may also be seen. If you look under a rock or in a hole you may even see a lobster. Again, don't reach in—their claws are very strong and can hurt. An octopus is another creature that may be seen in a hole or under a rock. If you scare it, it may even squirt its ink at you so that it can escape. Big fish may also be seen by the alert scuba diver. Manta rays sometimes glide by, flapping almost like a bird in flight. Keep a sharp eye out for barracuda and sharks. They will rarely try to hurt you, but it is a good idea to know when they are around and to be a little extra careful.

All it takes to scuba dive is to take a short course to learn the techniques and the safety rules that you must know, a little money to buy or rent the equipment, and a good location to see the right things. Maybe some day you will try this sport and become one of the new explorers of the strange world beneath our oceans.

Raise your hand now to let your teacher know that you have finished reading.

Mark down the time that your teacher tells you that it took to read the story. _____

Now answer the questions on the next page without looking back at the story.

Name _____

Date _____

Questions to Answer

1. When was scuba gear invented? _____

2. Who invented scuba equipment? _____

3. What sea creatures were mentioned in the story? _____

_____

_____

_____

4. Why does the story say that you need money? _____

_____

5 What sea creature is mentioned that you normally think of as something you find in the kitchen or bathroom? _____

6 What kind of eels are mentioned? _____

7. What moved like a bird? _____

The Most That I Think I Could Handle

DIRECTIONS: Read each phrase and fill in the blank following it to describe how much of each activity or experience you feel is the most you can handle.

Hours of homework in a day _____

Parties or dates during a weekend: parties _____   dates _____

Friends _____

Phone calls in a day _____

Boyfriends or girlfriends at one time _____

Chores at home in a day: how many? _____   how much time? _____

People living in my house at once _____

Slices of pizza to eat at one sitting _____

Pounds I could lift _____

Tests to take in one day _____

Number of people in an audience I could speak to _____

How long I would wait patiently for anything without complaining _____

Things That I Started but Didn't Finish

DIRECTIONS: For the next two or three days, keep track of the things you have not been able to complete and explain why. You may then be able to change your ways so that you can accomplish most things.

	Date	What I Didn't Finish	Why I Didn't Finish
IN SCHOOL			

	Date	What I Didn't Finish	Why I Didn't Finish
AT HOME			

LESSON 13

Learning to Say No

BACKGROUND FOR THE TEACHER

One of the hardest things for anyone, child or adult, to learn is to say no, particularly in a graceful manner. There are many needs that people have that makes saying no so difficult. There is the need to be loved, wanted, or needed, the need to be accepted by others, and the desire to avoid conflict. However, without the ability to say no, it is very easy to get caught up in situations that you would be better off not being involved in. Peer pressure—at any age—can lead to involvement in illegal acts and even serious crime, indulgence in alcohol and drugs, and general avoidance of responsibility. Not knowing how to say no can be one reason that a person gets involved in these things.

The same inability to say no can also lead to another seemingly less serious problem. A person can become loaded down with commitments and obligations to others. This seems at first glance to be a fairly minor problem, but this appearance can be deceptive. Overloading oneself with these obligations can lead to resentment toward the people who have asked these things of the person. Worse than that, it can lead to a physical and/or mental overload and possibly to the development of stress-related symptoms. There is only so much that each of us can handle at any given time. Should we go too far beyond our optimum load, we are likely to experience these problems and symptoms.

LESSON 13

Purpose: To help the children to say no so that they will not experience stress due to becoming overloaded with commitments and so that they will be able to resist peer pressure when necessary.

Materials Needed

Workbook Activities 13-1, 13-2, and 13-3

Directions

1. Use role playing to help develop strategies of how to say no and to give the children practice in saying no in situations similar to ones that they may experience.

2. Select the appropriate number of children to play the required roles and give them the situations. The children can then act out the situation as it might happen. Eight situations and the roles needed for them follow. For each situation, have the students act as if the person being asked says no poorly so that the other person is angry. Then have them act it out so that that person does not end up upset after getting a no answer.

- *Roles*—student, teacher
  Situation—The student asks to use the bathroom.
- *Roles*—student, teacher
  Situation—The student wants to be excused from homework because a relative will be visiting.
- *Roles*—two students
  Situation—One student wants the other's answers to last night's homework assignment.
- *Roles*—two students
  Situation—One student wants the other to join him or her in drinking, but the second student doesn't want to. The students are friends, though, so the refusal must be done so that they can remain friends. (This sequence can be repeated with the offer being for drugs instead.)
- *Roles*—parent, child
  Situation—The parent wants the child to go on an errand, but the child doesn't want to. The reason for refusing may be that the child is legitimately busy or simply that he or she doesn't want to go.
- *Roles*—parent, child
  Situation—The child wants the parent to drive him or her somewhere, but the parent refuses.
- *Roles*—two students
  Situation—One student is loaded down with work. His or her best friend asks the student to help him or her shop for clothes.

- *Roles*—parent, child

   Situation—The parent asks the child to help by staying home and babysitting for a younger sibling. The child wants to go out with friends, though, and doesn't want to babysit.

3. If it hasn't come out in the role playing, point out to the children that it is possible to have too many demands and responsibilities at a given time and that they may not be able to handle any more without undesirable effects. Help the children to understand that they should make clear to people that they can feel free to ask for help as long as they will accept the no that must be given at times. If the children have associations with people who are not willing to accept the negative answer and who will be upset and angry, they may have to reevaluate these people and their relationship with them.

Follow-up Suggestions

1. Discuss with the children how to say no to offers of drugs and alcohol and to peer pressure in general.

2. Have the children turn to Activity 13-1 in their workbooks. Students are asked to write their responses to the role-playing situations previously acted out.

3. Ask the children to use Activity 13-2 in the workbook to write a story entitled "The Girl (or Boy) Who Couldn't Say No."

4. Have the children fill in Activity 13-3 in the workbook, then discuss the students' responses together.

Learning to Say No

DIRECTIONS: How would you say no in the following situations? Write down what you would say. Try to say no so that the other person will not be angry, if possible.

1. You are a teacher who must say "no" to a student who asks to use the bathroom.

_____

_____

_____

_____

2. You are a teacher who must refuse a student special permission to be excused from homework during a relative's visit.

_____

_____

_____

_____

3. You are a student who refuses to give a classmate the answers to the homework assignment due that day.

_____

_____

_____

_____

4. You are a student who says no to an offer to join in drinking or taking drugs.

_____

_____

_____

5. You are a child who says no to a parent's request to go on an errand.

_____

_____

_____

6. You are a parent who refuses a child's request to be driven somewhere.

_____

_____

_____

7. You are a student with a lot of work to get done who says no when friends ask you to go with them on a shopping trip.

_____

_____

_____

8. You are a child who says no when your parents ask you to stay home and babysit for a younger brother or sister.

_____

_____

_____

Name _____

Date _____

The Girl (or Boy) Who Couldn't Say No

DIRECTIONS: Write a story entitled *The Girl (or Boy) Who Couldn't Say No*. If you need more space for the story, continue on the back of this sheet.

_____

_____

_____

_____

_____

_____

_____

_____

_____

_____

_____

_____

_____

_____

_____

_____

_____

When I've Said No

DIRECTIONS: Complete the following sentences. Be prepared to discuss your responses with the class.

Times I should have said no but didn't

_____

_____

_____

_____

_____

Times I said no and was glad I did

_____

_____

_____

_____

_____

Times I said no and wish I hadn't

_____

_____

_____

_____

LESSON 14

Assertiveness

BACKGROUND FOR THE TEACHER

A great deal of stress results from frustration, and a great deal of frustration comes from not being assertive. Studies have shown that a large percentage of the people who develop stress-related symptoms are rated very low on assertiveness. In the same way that laboratory rats that were not able to escape from stressful situations (and were thus helpless) developed symptoms, perhaps the people who do not have the skills to escape from their stressors also feel helplessness and develop the symptoms.

Since a lot of stress results from the feeling that we aren't getting our needs met, and since it is even worse if we feel that someone is taking advantage of us, it would help to be able to do something to allow our needs to be met and our rights to be asserted. Many people spend a lot of emotional energy being angry at how they have been treated, thinking what they should have said and planning how to get back at the other person. If you assert yourself in the first place, you can avoid much of this.

All of you have had times when you did not do anything in a situation and later wished that you had. Perhaps someone took advantage of you, pushed in front of you in line, or let it be known that they wanted a certain position before you were able to say that you wanted it. You may not have shown *assertive* behavior, but then wished that you had. We have already discussed learning to say no. That is one kind of assertive behavior. Many people are also not able to be assertive in getting what they want out of social situations. They may not be able to start a conversation or express emotions easily (see Lesson 21). These people may regret their lack of assertiveness because it is preventing their needs from being met. Many put themselves down later for not acting assertively or think of what would have been a good thing to say or do afterward, when it is too late. Developing assertive behavior will avoid this and can help lower anxiety about future situations because you will feel better able to handle them. Letting others take advantage of you and giving in to everyone else's wishes while putting aside your own can take their toll. You may not feel good about yourself, may worry a lot, and may even develop stress-related symptoms.

It can be very difficult for some people to be assertive, and we have always had mixed messages as to its desirability. We were taught to be polite, unselfish, and considerate, but were also taught the importance of success, winning, and status. Attaining the latter may often entail sacrificing the former. Women in particular are taught not to be assertive. Children are taught to obey adults and not to talk back. In school, the quiet, well-behaved, unaggressive child is the "ideal," and at work, employees are generally expected to mold to the system. Many times the behavior that is seen as desirable is not the behavior that leads to success.

Assertiveness entails standing up for your rights and wishes. An expression stated honestly, straightforwardly, and without guilt that does not try to step on others' rights is the goal. What is said, how it is said, and whether it is appropriate in that particular time and place are important. It must be emphasized that the understanding of the needs, wants, and rights of others is important. Assertive behavior is *not* aggressive behavior. It is fine to act in your own best interests and to stand up for yourself, and you should be able to express both your positive and negative feelings honestly, but this can be done without curtailing or ignoring others' rights. If what you do results in others' acting aggressively, your behavior may have been aggressive rather than assertive.

A point for you, the teacher, to realize is that once you have fostered assertive behavior, you must be prepared to accept this kind of conduct from the students, but you should make them aware of when their behavior is aggressive or inappropriate for the situation. The children should also realize that as they get assertive, others will react to them differently. There will be good results for themselves and many times things will turn out better. Sometimes there will be a result that they do not like or did not count on. Relationships will change when they change, particularly when they "upset the apple cart." They must be careful to be honest and to be aware of the feelings and rights of others. At times, it may even be better *not* to be assertive, depending on how they weigh the pros and cons.

Other aspects of assertiveness that may be dealt with are the ideas of expanding one's horizons and striving to improve, thinking positively, and taking risks (referring more to the "social" rather than "daredevil" connotation).

Be sure to emphasize the importance of believing in yourself. People pick up messages from your voice, gestures, posture, and other body language. If your messages, both verbal and nonverbal, say that you believe in yourself, others will too. If you show negative feelings about yourself, others get the message and will feel the same way.

Also realize that nonassertiveness reinforces in other people the manipulative behaviors that they are exhibiting and makes it likely that you will be frustrated again. Denying your own wishes when others express their wishes poorly (such as giving in when someone cries) also reinforces the other person's behavior.

NOTE: The following lesson is divided into three parts, each of which may be taught as a separate lesson.

LESSON 14

Purpose: To teach the children the components of assertive behavior and how to present themselves in the best manner so as to get the best responses.

Materials Needed

Workbook Activities 14-1 and 14-2

Part One: Components of Behavior

Directions

1. Do not tell the students what this lesson is about. Ask two students to leave the room for several minutes. Ask everyone else to turn to Activity 14-1 in their workbooks.

2. Explain that they are to take notes on the two students for each category both during the situations that they act out *and* when you yell at them afterward. Explain that "eye contact" refers to whether they looked at each other or you in the eye all, most of the time, some of the time, or never, or whether they looked down or away. Did they stare too hard at the other person? "Body posture" refers to whether they faced the other person directly, at a 90° angle, at a 180° angle, and so on. Did they stand erect or slump down? "Gestures" refers to how much they used their hands. "Facial expression" refers to frowns, smiles, clenched teeth, and so on. "Voice" refers to how loudly or softly they spoke, whether it was boring or expressive, and whether the tone of voice was friendly, angry, whining, and so on.

3. Have the two students return and give them two or three of the following situations to act out:

- You are returning a defective piece of merchandise to a store.
- You are in the middle of a long line at the movies when another person stands next to you and moves with the line, obviously intending to cut in.
- You (a student) want to tell the teacher that you believe your essay questions were not graded high enough.
- You would like to join another student working with a certain game, machine, or encyclopedia.

As the two students act these situations out, the other children in the class write notes on their behaviors and continue to do so when the skits are over and you begin to berate the students.

4. When the role playing is completed, tell the two students that they did not do the task correctly. Say that you asked them to speak with an accent and to speak for over 15 minutes (or anything else that you didn't really tell them), but that they didn't do as you said. If they do not respond, force an answer to your accusations. The purpose of this is to get their reactions in a more real situation

and to see if their response is different to an authority figure (you) than to each other.

5. After you get their responses (while the others continue their observations), explain to the two students that they did perform well and that you were noting behaviors of people as they interact and whether they were being assertive. (You may choose to include some of the material from your background section now to introduce the concept of assertiveness or you may save that material for later.)

6. Next, ask if the two responded to your unjust criticism in a way that was nonassertive (said nothing and accepted being wronged), assertive (stood up for themselves without forcing an unpleasant, adversarial, combative situation), or aggressive (reacted belligerently and in a manner that would probably cause you to lash out even more). This should lead to or continue your discussion of the differences between these types of behavior.

7. Discuss what types of behavior were exhibited by each child in the situations. Regarding eye contact, it should be noted that looking at a person is generally interpreted as more sincere. Looking down or away may be seen as a lack of confidence and of giving the other person the upper hand. Too much eye contact can make the other person uncomfortable and may seem to be forced and even aggressive and threatening. You need to find a happy medium, but many people do not show enough eye contact. Also point out that "comfortable" eye contact differs in different cultures and may be different when it is between a younger and older person or the opposite sexes. Being aware of eye contact can help you improve and enhance your ability to relate to others and get what is desired.

Regarding posture, many people speak while turning away. Some only turn their head toward the person they are addressing. Turning toward a person (at least a good part of the way) may help and is an easy habit to change once aware of not doing it. Whether you are seated while the other stands may imply a superior/subordinate position. You may want to literally "stand up" when trying to stand up for yourself. Moving away also implies taking a subordinate position, as does slouching. These, too, can be remedied easily.

Also mention how gestures and other body language can add to your message and its effectiveness, when not done in excess. Facial expression gives messages and can be worked on as well, as can vocal inflection, tone of voice, and volume. Whining, yelling, whispering, frowning, smiling, and the like, all add to or take away from what you are actually saying. How close a person stands also has meaning. You may get so close that you make someone feel uncomfortable or threatened, or may be so far away that no feeling of closeness can develop. Moving closer (without going too close) may help a situation at times. (Interpretations of distance may also differ in different cultures, by the way.)

8. Since the two children selected to act out the scenes have been scrutinized so carefully, point out that most children show the same behaviors and that you were only trying to show how some may give the wrong message and may need to be changed.

Part Two: Continuation of Distinguishing Assertive, Nonassertive, and Aggressive Behavior

Directions

1. In order to get children thinking and responding assertively and to help distinguish among nonassertive, assertive, and aggressive behavior, use role playing again. Have two children act out each of the following situations in *each* manner. Along with each situation, an example has been given of what might be done:

- Your dad had promised to take you bowling this weekend. It's Sunday, at noon, and he still hasn't brought it up. *Examples:* Nonassertive—You walk by him, say hello, and go to your room. Aggressive—You start yelling that he never takes you anywhere, never keeps promises, and doesn't love you. You say that he promised to take you bowling, but probably won't because he bowls so badly. Assertive—You remind him that you had plans to bowl this weekend and that this afternoon is the only time that you can still go. You also let him know that you were looking forward to it and were disappointed that he had not mentioned it yet.

- You are in the meat market waiting to place an order. It is your turn, but two other people are served who came after you. One had simply called out her order. The other went ahead because the butcher came up to him and asked what he wanted. *Examples:* Nonassertive—You do nothing or you mumble under your breath that they haven't been fair and you walk out. Aggressive—You yell, "Am I invisible?" or "What a store. Don't you idiots even know who's next?" Assertive—You speak up in a clear voice, but not abusively, that you have waited your turn, which has been passed over twice, and would like to be served.

- There is a kickball game in the schoolyard before school begins and you would like to play. *Examples:* Nonassertive—You walk over and hang around, hoping to be asked to play. Aggressive—You walk over and say, "I'm playing. Whose side am I on?" or you run onto the field and catch a ball and throw it to first. Assertive—As one team goes to field and the other gets up, you ask who the captains are and tell them that you would like to play. You ask if they can fit you in and offer to find another player to even the sides if that is a problem.

2. You may want the children to role play even more situations. If so, see Follow-up Suggestions.

Part Three: Speaking and Listening

Directions

1. Have each child come to the front of the class and speak from 30 to 60 seconds on any given topic. You might even have the following topics (or any others) folded up on pieces of paper and selected from a bag:

- Persuade the class to buy a product, such as a specific automobile or laundry detergent.
- Tell why reading is such an important school subject to master.
- Invite someone to go somewhere with you and make it sound very appealing.
- Explain why you would make a good class president.

2. Try to foster fluency and ease of speaking. Have the rest of the class note pauses ("ers" and "uhs"), posture, voice, expression, volume, speed, and so on. Each of these can be improved with practice. Emphasize how difficult it can be to speak in front of others and how the children should be supportive of each speaker.

3. Because assertiveness involves interaction, and one of its aims is to get a point across or an action taken without infringing on or upsetting others, listening is an important skill. Repeat the same exercise as in Step 1, but this time make it a two-person dialogue and allow for evaluation of both the speaker *and* the listener. Have the other children note whether listening was done attentively and with verbal, postural, visual, and gestural cues to indicate the listener's attentiveness and reactions. Two students might act out the following:

- Two students discuss whose car is better.
- A child complains to a record store manager that no album was in the sealed jacket just purchased.
- Two students compare notes on two different movies (or even the same one) they have just seen.
- A wife and husband talk about dividing up the chores.

Follow-up Suggestions

1. Have the children do Activity 14-2 in their workbooks. They are to describe how they would handle the situation nonassertively, aggressively, and assertively.

2. Ask the children to keep track of the instances in which they acted assertively and to share them with the class. Be sure they share both the good and bad results of acting in this manner so they can learn from each other's experiences.

3. Discuss with the students what the proper reaction is to others' aggressive behavior. One reaction is to let the other person get it out of his or her system and calm down. Don't take it personally, because the other person may be upset in general, not at you. If you respond with aggression, it may make the situation worse. If you are wrong, admit it. You might mention that you realize your error angered them, but that their reaction was also wrong. If you are not wrong, you can acknowledge that you realize the other person is upset, but that he or she is not considering you or your feelings at all by attacking you in this manner. After this, avoid further immediate contact.

If someone is indirectly attacking you, as with snide remarks, you can ask that person to clarify what he or she means. This type of confrontation can also be used in response to dirty looks and insulting gestures. Realize, of course, if you choose these tactics, that although things will be out in the open, there is also a chance of more explosive or aggressive confrontation. This is also true when someone ignores you instead of acting out his or her aggressiveness other ways.

When others act aggressively it is not always possible to say something that will straighten things out. You may need to decide at times to really work at talking it out or working out a compromise, or even walking away or fighting. Neither walking away nor fighting should be done before you have tried to establish what messages each of you was sending and have tried to work things out, because neither tactic will get rid of the problem.

Assertiveness

DIRECTIONS: Fill in the following chart for the two students acting out the scenes. Complete a different chart for each situation role played.

	First Person		Second Person	
	during the scene	when teacher yells	during the scene	when teacher yells
eye contact				
body posture				
distance				
body contact				
gestures				
facial expression				
voice				

Name _____   ACTIVITY 14–2

Date _____

Three Responses

DIRECTIONS: Read the description of each situation, then write about how each could be handled in a nonassertive, aggressive, and assertive manner.

1. You are studying for a test and your brother is blasting the stereo in the next room.

   nonassertive _____

   _____

   _____

   aggressive _____

   _____

   _____

   assertive _____

   _____

   _____

2. You get the bill in a restaurant and have been charged for French fries, which were not ordered, *and* have also been overcharged $1.50.

   nonassertive _____

   _____

   _____

   aggressive _____

   _____

   _____

   assertive _____

   _____

   _____

3. You are eating dinner in a restaurant, and a man sitting near you lights up a smelly cigar, which annoys you and ruins your meal.

nonassertive _____

_____

_____

aggressive _____

_____

_____

assertive _____

_____

_____

4. You are new to the school and would like to meet some of your new schoolmates. You see a group of children in the schoolyard talking.

nonassertive _____

_____

_____

aggressive _____

_____

_____

assertive _____

_____

_____

5. The person sitting behind you at a movie keeps kicking your seat.

nonassertive _____

_____

_____

aggressive _____

_____

_____

_____

assertive _____

_____

_____

_____

6. Your teacher is writing notes on the chalkboard and you can't see them clearly.

nonassertive _____

_____

_____

aggressive _____

_____

_____

assertive _____

_____

_____

7. You like only rare meat. You order a hamburger very rare and it comes very well done.

nonassertive _____

_____

_____

aggressive _____

_____

_____

assertive _____

_____

_____

Handling Anger

BACKGROUND FOR THE TEACHER

There are many things that can cause anger in a person, and different people get angry at different things. For that matter, the same occurrence may anger a given person at a given time, but on another day or in another setting or mood, it may not cause anger. The *social setting* may be an important determinant of how anger is expressed because there may be written or unwritten guidelines as to what is acceptable. For example, anger expressed on the football field or at an open hearing on proposed legislation will be less likely to be frowned upon than anger expressed in a classroom. Each person has his or her own code as to what he or she believes is acceptable, which will be based on past experience and his or her own personality. This will, of course, change over time as others react to a person's behavior.

One general cause of anger is *frustration*. This generally occurs early in a child's life because it is necessary for adults to frustrate a child's natural (and immature) desires as the child is socialized and taught acceptable behavior. The child learns that he or she cannot have and do everything that he or she desires whenever he or she wants it. This type of frustration may be even more of a problem for personalities who have a "live for today" and "I want what I want, when I want it" attitude. This attitude can be furthered by permissive parents who want to give their children the things they have missed out on themselves. This may postpone many of the frustrations that result from the socializing process, but at some point these children will be faced with the reality that in the real world not everybody is willing to give them and let them do anything they want.

Another cause of frustration is the fact that there are a great number of people in our country who are excluded from many of our society's niceties and luxuries for racial or economic reasons. This is particularly frustrating due to the fact that television accentuates the upper-middle-class lifestyle that is foreign and out of reach (yet obviously has its appeal) to a large part of the population.

The anger that results may be shown in temper tantrums, yelling, or screaming, depression, or physical expression, either aggressive and antisocial outlets or socially acceptable ones, such as sports. It is also possible to be angry without showing it in one of the aforementioned ways. People may not even be aware of their anger. What some people call being "fed up," "sick of it," or "disappointed" may actually be anger that they are failing to acknowledge and express. One reason that anger may be denied is that children are taught to control anger and may interpret "controlling" it to mean denying that it exists. (See Lesson 21.) By not realizing you are angry and not allowing any expression of it, emotion is denied. This can lead to or be a symptom of further losing touch with emotion in general.

There is much disagreement on whether letting out anger is desirable. Obviously, we can fault the two extremes of unchecked temper outbursts and absolute failure to show emotion, but there is a great deal of territory between them. In general, it probably makes sense to at least express that you are angry. By feeling that you at least said something, you may avoid being upset with yourself later for failing to say anything. You really don't want to be in the position of saying "I should have..." and "If only I had...." By stating your anger, you do have a chance of getting a desired result from the target of anger.

Whether or not a person feels in control may be an important factor in whether the anger's effects are bad or not. This is not a simple problem. Physical aggressiveness may or may not get your desired end. Verbal aggressiveness runs the same risk, as does even the expression that you are angry. The target (if a person) may become more angered and further confrontation may result. The letting out of anger is said to have a cathartic effect. The reaction it receives is an important factor, however. Also, if you let out anger consistently, feeling that this has worked, it may become viewed as the only way to deal with anger and with the situations. This can lead to a self-fulfilling prophecy ("I feel better by letting out my anger because I believe I will. Therefore, I let it out. Then, I think I feel better.") That's great as far as "feeling better" is concerned, but it may not always be appropriate and can lead to other problems. This cathartic effect is certainly negated if you then feel guilty about having let it out.

Another point needs to be made about letting out your anger in an aggressive manner. This may become the normal reaction to situations. Also, the cause of the anger has not been dealt with and the problem is not solved, so the situation and the anger may then recur. Of course, throwing a tantrum may get a person his or her way. The situation hasn't been eased, however, for the future. Tantrums are, of course, not the only way to let it out. Punching a pillow or squeezing a rubber ball are possibly more desirable, as may be fantasizing about doing the aggressive things that you would like to do (such as beating up the person). However, it must be remembered that you are then still reacting aggressively to anger.

Another suggested way of dealing with anger is to talk things out. This has the possible pitfall of rehearsing the anger and dragging it out even longer. In other words, it may not always be appropriate to talk things out because the anger can't dissipate quickly.

Thus, it is not really possible to say whether to let out anger or not. Points can be made both ways.

If anger is to be let out, there are a number of possible outlets other than outbursts of temper. One is for the energy to be channeled into a constructive activity leading to the accomplishment of some goal. For example, the anger over being in a traffic accident may be channeled into working to get a stop sign put on the dangerous corner.

Sports are another way to let out anger in a socially acceptable manner. Football, hockey, wrestling, and boxing are obvious outlets. Hitting a baseball and knocking down bowling pins may also do, as may lifting weights, running, or any other physical activity.

Humor may be an outlet, too. Anger may be let out by making fun (particularly of the target of the anger) or even by laughing at something else. You, the teacher, may be able to use this aspect at times. If you can get the two parties into a situation of poking fun and get some laughter, you may help ease some of the tension. Put-down sessions, where two children say bad things about each other, are also a way of their letting out anger without actual physical aggression. They also often lead to a good insult or put-down and laughter, which then may ease things a bit. Realize also that the longer the period of time after initial anger without physical aggression, the less chance it will occur.

Letting out anger and channeling it are not the only ways to handle anger. You may first recognize that you are feeling angry and then decide what you are angry about (the real reason, not necessarily what you say at first) and then decide how to deal with it. Verbalizing what you feel may help (but say it, rather than yell it). This verbalization is not really the same as letting it out because you are trying to control the anger. An important point to remember is that even when you are sure you are right, you can't necessarily get others to agree and to accede to your wishes. Compromise may be necessary, with a solution somewhere between what each of the parties wants. Your assertiveness techniques may help, too.

Physically, there are things you may do. As you start to feel that powerful physical "blood-boiling" feeling that goes with anger, you should recall the relaxation techniques that you have learned. Remember, you now know how to slow down your body. Check your breathing and take a few deep breaths and then do your slowing-down relaxation techniques. This will also help because you have taken a moment out to think about your body instead of what was upsetting you. Walking around the block, counting to ten, or doing some exercise are also used by some people to take their minds off things long enough to begin to calm down. Another suggestion is to try to understand the other person's side and to reappraise the situation. You may see why the person acted as he or she did and may even see that you are not totally right.

Realize also that once you are using your relaxation exercises regularly, it may take more to bring you to the boiling point. Your body will be naturally calmer and you may be "mellower" in general.

LESSON 15

Purpose: To show the children several ways to deal with anger. (As there is a great deal of disagreement on the pros and cons of each, no "correct" way is given. It is important to emphasize how the relaxation techniques may help.)

Materials Needed

Workbook Activities 15-1 and 15-2

Directions

1. You do not have to do much to introduce this lesson because most of the children are very familiar with getting angry. Simply ask them to turn to Activity 15-1 in their workbooks and fill in the chart.

2. The workbook activity should easily lead to a discussion of what kinds of things get the children angry and how they react. Once this has begun, use the background material to guide the points to be made.

3. Try some role playing, particularly as it may be the first time some children will have experienced different ways of expressing and dealing with anger. Let the children decide on the situations they would like to role play, incorporating the following reactions to anger. After each situation, discuss with the children their reactions and the pros and cons of each child's behavior.

- You and another child let out your anger in tantrums.
- You have a tantrum while another child doesn't.
- You tell another person that you are angry and why.
- You show how humor could ease the situation.
- You and the other child work out a compromise.
- You show how relaxation techniques may be used.

4. Now have the children read the situations found in Activity 15-2 in their workbooks. Ask the students to write different ways of dealing with the anger.

Follow-up Suggestion

Angry situations occur often, so remind the children of ways to handle the anger and the situation. After they have a chance to try out their new techniques, let the children describe how they acted and how they tried to handle the anger. Were they successful? Was it an improvement from before? What didn't work?

Name _____

Date _____

The Last Ten Times I Have Been Angry

DIRECTIONS: Fill in the following chart.

With Whom I Was Angry	Why I Was Angry	What I Did When I Got Angry	What the Other Person Did After I Got Angry
1.			
2.			
3.			
4.			
5.			
6.			
7.			
8.			
9.			
10.			

Date _____

What Would You Do?

DIRECTIONS: How would you act in each of the following situations that might get you angry?

1. You and another child want to use the same toy at the same time.

_____

_____

_____

_____

2. Someone insults you in front of your friends.

_____

_____

_____

_____

3. Your teacher makes you do something that you don't want to do.

_____

_____

_____

_____

4. You fail a math test.

_____

_____

_____

_____

LESSON 16

Waiting and Patience

BACKGROUND FOR THE TEACHER

Many children are already rushing around all the time and suffering stress as a result of an inability to wait patiently in the many situations that call for waiting in any normal day. The following lesson highlights the fact that waiting can be a problem for many children and points out that the time saved in rushing may not be worth the emotional price.

127

LESSON 16

Purpose: To show the children that the time saved in rushing may not be worth the emotional price.

Materials Needed

> stopwatch
> paper
> pencil
> Workbook Activity 16-1

Directions

1. Start the lesson without mentioning the topic. Use a stopwatch to note when you begin. Simply stand in front of the class and do not say anything. As soon as someone begins to fidget or exhibit impatient behaviors or calls out something, record the time it occurred and the child's name on a piece of paper. You might distinguish between the start of impatient behavior for an individual and when that same person actually confronts you verbally. Do this for three to five minutes. There should be enough recorded instances within that time frame; if not, use your own discretion.

2. Now explain that this is going to be a lesson on waiting and patience and ask if anyone knows what you were doing. The children will probably now realize, but if not, tell them. Explain that they know you are the teacher and that you have lessons prepared for them. Point out that they knew that you would tell them what to do but that many did not have the patience to let you begin when you were ready to begin. Let them know how short a time it was (in minutes and seconds) that each could not wait. Explain how short the entire experiment was.

3. Have the children turn to the chart on Activity 16-1 in their workbooks. After they have completed the activity, get from the students a list of the situations in which they find it difficult to wait. Some possibilities include:

- Waiting in lines at supermarkets or movies
- Waiting for elevators
- Waiting for the traffic light to turn green while walking or driving
- Waiting for trains or buses
- Waiting a turn in a game
- Waiting to be called on to give an answer

Discuss what behavior they exhibit in the situations in which they find waiting difficult. Elicit whether there are any constructive activities that may be done while waiting, such as reading, doing homework, planning out a day, thinking over a problem, or writing a letter. You might discuss the relationship between patience and type-A behavior (see Lesson 18). Also mention how some people are so impatient that they do not even let others finish their sentences.

4. Use a short math example to point out how impatience and rushing do not necessarily rectify a situation. Put the following problem on the chalkboard:

> What is the difference between the time it takes to travel 25 miles if you speed at 65 miles per hour instead of going at 55 miles per hour?

(Solution)

At 55 m.p.h.: $\dfrac{25}{55} = \dfrac{x}{60}$ $\quad 55x = 1500 \quad x = 1500 \div 55 = 27$ minutes

At 65 m.p.h.: $\dfrac{25}{65} = \dfrac{x}{60}$ $\quad 65x = 1500 \quad \sim \; \dot{=} \; 1500 \div 65 = 23$ minutes

Thus, by going at 65 m.p.h., you save *four minutes.* Big deal!

Follow-up Suggestion

Have the children share strategies that have worked while they're waiting. Activities, thoughts, and statements they repeat to themselves are all acceptable.

Times That I Find It Hard to Be Patient

DIRECTIONS: Complete the following chart.

WHAT HAPPENS	HOW I ACT

LESSON 17

How People Act as a Result of Stress

BACKGROUND FOR THE TEACHER

Many people, as a result of stress or anxiety, choose a certain way to act. They act this way in almost all situations and thus avoid the need to deal with each situation individually. These behaviors include the "rebel," the "tough guy (or girl)," the "loner," "Mr. (or Ms.) Wonderful," the "workaholic," the "do-gooder," the "scapegoat," the "conformist," the "optimist," the "pessimist," and the "put-off."

LESSON 17

Purpose: To show the children several styles of behavior chosen as a result of stress.

Materials Needed

Workbook Activities 17-1 and 17-2

Directions

1. Ask the children who would agree with the following statements:

   a. If something can go wrong, it will.
   b. Nothing ever works out for me, no matter what I do.
   c. Somehow, everything always turns out right.
   d. Never put things off.
   e. I always put things off to do them another time.
   f. Never break any rules.
   g. I break every rule I can.

   After getting the children's responses, go over each one and how it indicates the answer of an optimist or pessimist (a, b, c), a procrastinator (d, e), or a do-gooder or rebel (f, g).

2. Next have the children turn to Activity 17-1 in their workbooks and read the selection either together or silently. Then ask the children to answer the questions in Activity 17-2.

Answers to Activity 17-2

Part One

1. rules
2. freedom
3. puts things off for later
4. you weighed all the possibilities
5. the worst will happen
6. our conscience
7. optimist and pessimist
8. withdrawal, being alone, acting as scapegoat
9. do the right things
10. desires
11. he or she has all the facts
12. he or she misses out on some good opportunities

Part Two

1. push something out of your mind

2. to do something too much
3. a person who always expects the best
4. a person who always expects the worst
5. to interfere with
6. react
7. a way of acting, strategy
8. looking back in time
9. to pull away or back
10. a person who stays to himself or herself
11. answers will vary, but an example is going home and picking on your little brother
12. to do what others do
13. good and bad points

Part Three

1. it was a good decision at the time and you couldn't know everything that was going to occur in the future
2. he or she worries over a longer period of time
3. he or she rushes to do things too quickly
4. he or she doesn't decide which ones are right to break; he or she just breaks them all
5. a person who works all the time and is only concerned with work

Follow-up Suggestions

1. Use the information given in Activity 17-1 to spark discussions on the various types of behavior exhibited by people under stress.

2. Create your own situations and have the children act out or write about how different types would act. Here are two examples:

- The teacher leaves the room for an important phone call. She puts one child in charge of the class. How would the do-gooder and the rebel each act while in charge of the class?

- The teacher announces that there is a test on the first four science chapters next week. What would the "optimist," "pessimist," "procrastinator," and "do-gooder" each do?

How People Act as a Result of Stress

DIRECTIONS: Read the following information. Be prepared to discuss it with your class. All of us have wants and needs. We also have a conscience that tries to prevent us from doing whatever we want, whenever we want if it would *impinge* on, or interfere with, other people. We know it would not be right to force our wishes on other people. We do, however, still have our needs and may suffer anxiety and stress over them. We may *respond*, or react, to these desires in different ways.

Some people ignore their conscience and act exactly the way they feel like acting, even when it may hurt others. They may act in an inconsiderate, mean, selfish, and even criminal manner. These people just cannot handle the stress of their conscience acting, and so they have learned to ignore it. They may suffer in the end, though, if their conscience starts getting control again, and they can certainly suffer when they are stopped by others (including the police) from acting as they wish. They also lose out in that others often dislike them and they don't get the support and love of others.

At the other extreme are those people who get anxious about their desires and try not to admit that they are there. They become totally ruled by their conscience. These people will never do anything that may be thought of as "bad." They will *go overboard* in trying to do the right thing. They get to school and work early, stay late, won't curse, won't drink, and won't do anything "bad." They will also look down on anyone else who does these things. The problem for these people is that they have the same desires as other people, but are always fighting their conscience. They may be disliked by others for trying to be so good, and may also miss out on many of the fun things in life because they label many things as "bad" that are not really harmful.

Another way that people react can be seen in the rebel. The rebel is so anxious about his or her freedom that he or she breaks rules just for the sake of breaking them, rather than deciding which ones he or she should break. Rules, then, rule a rebel's life, too, but in the opposite way.

Do you know anyone who fits any of these descriptions?

People also get anxious over having to make decisions. There are three ways that people may show this in an unhealthy way. The first is when someone is always trying to be an *optimist*. This person says that things will turn out all right. It is good to have a positive attitude, but if you act this way in every situation and don't do the things necessary to solve the situations, it can be a problem. This type of person may rush things, and just hope they will work out, but may not do the things necessary to try to ensure that they do work out. He or she may say, "It will all work out" and then trust that luck will get him or her through things when it really takes hard work and planning. The optimist just wants to get things over with and reduce his or her anxiety, even though mistakes may be made.

The opposite of the optimist is the *pessimist*. This person always expects the worst and believes that things will not work out. He or she says that it doesn't matter what you do, bad luck will get you somehow. The pessimist is also anxious about decisions and likes to avoid them. One *tactic* that the pessimist may use to avoid making a decision is saying that he or she needs all the facts, even if they are not available. The pessimist may make fewer mistakes because he or she doesn't rush into a decision, but he or she also misses out on many good opportunities by being *too* cautious.

There is a third reaction to the stress of making decisions. We can call these people "put-offs." This reaction is called procrastination, or taking your time about doing something and putting it off for some time later. This person suffers stress both from making a decision and trying to avoid it. The "put-off" says, "I'll get to it tomorrow" or "I'll do it soon." This person will even avoid thinking about the decision. This is a real problem, though, since the procrastinator usually gives him- or herself even more stress. This person still has the decision to make but now he or she worries about it longer.

There are a few more important things to be said about decisions. Many people give themselves much more stress over a decision than it really deserves. They can put it off and worry for an even longer time. They then have the stress as they are making the decision and also while they are doing what they decided to do. Then they give themselves stress for a third time over the same decision (and it may have been only an unimportant decision) after they have made it and they start to worry about the results and whether it was the correct decision. So they can have stress before, during, and after the decision.

This brings us to another important point. Many people suffer a great deal of stress by using *hindsight,* or looking back at a decision that they have made. It may not have worked out perfectly, so they begin to think that they have made a bad decision. They put themselves down for making a bad decision and worry about how things didn't turn out well. This is a foolish way to act. *If* they made that decision after looking at all the facts that were available, weighing the *pros and cons* and deciding that this was the best decision, then it was a good decision. This is true even if things turned out badly. It was still the best decision at the time and knowing what was known. Nobody can see the future. Things happen that we couldn't have figured on. All of the facts are not always available. Instead of saying "I am a bad person for making this decision" or sitting around worrying about how badly things turned out, the person should just decide what he or she can do (make another decision) to make the situation better and then go ahead and do it. REMEMBER: If you made an intelligent decision based on the facts, it was a good decision *at the time,* even if it turned out badly. Then just go ahead and straighten things out.

People do still other things when they get anxious. Some people *withdraw,* or pull away, from others. They become *loners* and stay to themselves. Other people choose *scapegoats;* they find someone or something to take frustrations out on. Being a bully is an example of this kind of behavior. Some people are afraid to have any problems with people so they become "Mr. (or Ms.) Wonderful." They never argue or do anything to have problems with other people, even when they may want to and think they are right! The "tough guy (or girl)" does the opposite. This person is anxious about things, too, but has decided to always act tough so it looks like he or she is never anxious and is in control. This person won't ever give in to his or her feelings and act the way he or she might like to.

Some people become *conformists*. They decide to just go along with everyone else. That way, they never have to make big decisions about what they really want or what they like. They let everyone else decide how they should dress and act. They will have problems both in relating to others (since they don't let themselves be themselves), and in being alone (because they then have to make their own decisions). Other people are anxious over how they feel about themselves or over being with people, so they may become real "go-getters" or "workaholics" or "brown-noses." They may come to school or work early, always ask if they can help and do more and try to butter up the teacher or boss. They usually spend all their time and energy on school work or at work. They are usually anxious about being with people or anxious in general. They also may have a need to prove themselves or to compensate (make up for) for something about which they are insecure (such as a very short person who tries to be tough). They may do well in school or work when they act this way, but they may not be liked by other people and others may not talk to them. They may then suffer from loneliness and be unhappy. They are also so buried in their work that they miss out on many of the other enjoyable things that life has to offer, such as friends, social life, and play-time activities.

A real problem may arise when people turn to alcohol, drugs, or cigarettes to try to deal with anxiety. They aren't solving any of the problems and will feel just as bad about them when the effects of the alcohol or drugs wear off. They then need to get high again and try to "forget" again. New problems can be created by the alcohol and drugs as well, while the old problems remain.

Questions on Anxiety

DIRECTIONS FOR PART ONE: Complete the following questions concerning the story you have just read.

1. A rebel's life ends up being ruled by _____.

2. A rebel is anxious about his or her _____.

3. A procrastinator is someone who _____

   _____.

4. A decision is good if _____

   _____.

5. A pessimist expects _____.

6. What prevents us from always giving in to our desires? _____

7. The opposite extremes of worry over decisions are _____

   _____   _____.

8. What are some ways in which people react to anxiety? _____

   _____

9. People who are ruled by their conscience always try to _____

   _____.

10. People ruled by their conscience are anxious about their _____.

11. A pessimist will not make a decision until _____

    _____.

12. Because the pessimist is too cautious, _____

    _____.

DIRECTIONS FOR PART TWO: Find these words in the story and tell what they mean.

1. suppress _____

2. go overboard _____

3. optimist _____

4. pessimist _____

5. impinge on _____

6. respond _____

7. tactic _____

8. hindsight _____

9. withdraw _____

10. loner _____

11. an example of scapegoating _____

_____

12. conform _____

13. pros and cons _____

DIRECTIONS FOR PART THREE: Read each question and answer one by inference or by drawing a conclusion.

1. If you thought you made an intelligent decision but it turned out badly, why is it foolish to think badly of yourself? _____

_____

2. A procrastinator has more stress than others because _____

_____   _____

3. Why would an optimist make many mistakes? _____

_____

4. A rebel breaks all the rules. How could we say, then, that a rebel is really ruled by the rules?

_____

5. What is a workaholic? _____

_____

Type-A Behavior

BACKGROUND FOR THE TEACHER

According to some researchers, type-A personalities have been shown to have more stress than others. People who exhibit this type of behavior also are much more likely to have cardiovascular problems. Some studies with adults showed higher incidence of heart problems in this type of person. This data is still being evaluated, however. There has also been evidence that children who exhibit this type of personality may have physiological differences developing, such as increased cholesterol levels. Type-A people would probably do well to try to change their behavior, and to take more time out for relaxation and to try to lower their body's arousal level.

Some characteristics of type-A behavior are explosive speech; doing things rapidly; impatience; trying to do several things at once; monopolizing conversation and forcing it to topics of self-interest; inability to relax; failure to observe surroundings; need to acquire things; no free time; no hobbies; trying to do more in less time; a need to challenge others (particularly other type-A people); belief that success is due to being faster than others at doing things; and nervous tics, gestures, and habits. Type-A people also seem to like to feel "in control."

This lesson is simply aimed at helping the students identify whether they have signs of this type of behavior. They should be made aware of its potential danger and that they need to relax more.

NOTE: Some recent studies have challenged the idea that type-A people run any greater health risk than others. There are those who argue for each view. This material is included to enable you to recognize type-A styles and behavior. You may follow the research and decide for yourself on which side of the controversy your views lie.

LESSON 18

Purpose: To help the children identify signs of type-A behavior in themselves and others.

Materials Needed

Workbook Activity 18-1

Directions

1. Have the children answer the questionnaire on Activity 18-1 in their workbooks. After they have circled the value from 1 to 5 that shows the extent that each statement applies to them, go over their responses. The questions have purposely been mixed so that at times type-A behavior has a value of 1 and at other times 5.

Then have the children add up their scores. A score of 105 shows the most tendency toward type-A behavior, while 21 shows the least. Emphasize that the score only shows whether someone seems to be this fast-paced type of person or whether he or she pays more attention to relaxing.

2. Use the background material to discuss type-A behavior with the children.

Follow-up Suggestion

Have each child choose at least one type-A behavior to work on changing. Have the children share with the class what they did to change it and how it worked for them. For example, a child who answered question 5 with a value of five may decide to force himself or herself to eat slowly and make a promise to sit at the table doing nothing for five minutes if he or she rushes the meal. Even though the child is artificially changing behavior, point out that at least he or she is trying out the calmer behavior, and that's a start! Also, if students "punish" themselves for the type-A behavior (as in sitting for five extra minutes) they will at least notice that the undesired behavior occurred and may think about it next time *before* they do it.

Name _____

Date _____

Type-A Behavior

DIRECTIONS: Read each of the following 21 statements. Then check only one of the five boxes next to each statement.

1. I speak	loudly — 5	— 4	— 3	— 2	softly — 1
2. If people are talking and the topic doesn't interest me, I	listen and try to join in later — 1	listen but don't join in — 2	pretend to listen but think of other things — 3	butt in and say anything — 4	try to change the conversation to something I like — 5
3. I have	many hobbies and interests — 1	— 2	— 3	— 4	few hobbies and interests — 5
4. I _____ wait in lines easily.	can — 1	— 2	— 3	— 4	can't — 5
5. I _____ move, eat, drive, walk, etc. quickly	never — 1	— 2	— 3	— 4	always — 5
6. I care more about *getting* things than doing things	a lot — 5	— 4	— 3	— 2	not at all — 1
7. I am always in a rush and can't seem to get everything done	yes — 5	— 4	— 3	— 2	no — 1
8. I am too busy for relaxation, exercise, etc.	never — 1	— 2	— 3	— 4	always — 5
9. Lately I get more and more done in less and less time	applies to me — 5	— 4	— 3	— 2	does not apply — 1
10. I believe that one of my strengths is my ability to get things done more quickly than others	yes — 5	— 4	— 3	— 2	no — 1
11. It is important that I have a lot of money, things, etc.	very — 5	— 4	— 3	— 2	not at all — 1

Name _____

Date _____

Type-A Behavior

12. It is important (in judging other's success) how much money and things they have	not at all — 1	2	3	4	very — 5
13. When I relax I	feel guilty because I could be doing something con-structive — 5	am still a little fidgety — 4	sometimes relax and sometimes can't — 3	mostly relax — 2	block out everything — 1
14. While doing one thing I ____ am doing or thinking about another	never — 1	2	3	4	always — 5
15. I ____ finish other people's sentences or wish they would hurry up	always — 5	4	3	2	never — 1
16. I ____ challenge and confront others	like to — 5	4	3	2	don't like to — 1
17. I clench my fists	never — 1	2	3	4	always — 5
18. I have tics	often — 5	4	3	2	never — 1
19. I stutter	often — 5	4	3	2	never — 1
20. I grind my teeth	never — 1	2	3	4	often — 5
21. I tense my jaw	never — 1	2	3	4	often — 5

Add up the total in all the boxes you have checked. The numbers are in the lower part of each box. A score of 21 is the lowest and indicates that you do not exhibit much Type-A behavior. A score of 105 is the highest and shows a high incidence of Type-A behavior. The closer to each of these two scores your score falls indicates which way you lean.

LESSON 19

Making Friends and Developing Confidants

BACKGROUND FOR THE TEACHER

Making new friends requires skill that many children lack. Because friends and confidants can be a tremendous buffer against stress, everyone should have at least one. Through the following lesson, the children will begin to notice how, where, and when others have made new friends.

LESSON 19

Purpose: To show the children some of the behaviors that may lead to meeting and making new friends.

Materials Needed

Workbook Activities 19-1 and 19-2

Directions

1. Begin the lesson by having the children complete Activity 19-1 in their workbooks, then discuss what they wrote. If the following points do not come out during the discussion, you might bring them up:

- Friendships are often built upon playing or doing things together, having something in common, sharing, being able to talk, being pleasant, helping other people and being able to depend on them as well, trust, understanding, and compassion. The opposite of each of these factors is what often causes friendships to end.
- Friends have some kind of ongoing contact.
- Other characteristics are feeling comfortable, seeing the best *and* worst of each other, accepting the bad side of the other person, and accepting his or her refusals.
- There is usually some feeling of commitment to each other.

2. Now have the children complete the "Situations and Places Where I Have Met a New Friend" section in Activity 19-2. Follow up with a discussion of their answers. If it does not come out in the discussion, you might add some comments on the types of strategies that can be used in entering a strange group and in making friends. For example:

- *Put yourself in an area of interaction.* You want to be in a location and situation conducive to meeting people. A club, school team, hobby group, joining a gym, public park or pool, theater group, and exercise class are examples. Just going to a park where other children will be playing is a possibility if it's a safe place.

Once at the location or in the situation, skill is necessary in knowing whether caution or direct action is more appropriate. Just putting yourself in the situation may allow a cautious approach to work in that others may take the initial step. If not, it is possible to take direct action and approach a group or individual and ask whether you might participate. Friendly behavior can go a long way. The behavior itself is not enough, however, as it is important how it is expressed and how it is interpreted. It may be necessary for the child to try to learn to be more outgoing. It may also be necessary to learn to stop coming on so strong. Some skills that are beneficial are being approving, helpful, and supportive. It is important in forming friendships that people believe you are sincerely interested in them. Tact is important. Showing interest in others and in their own interests is important. You must learn to be a little less self-centered at times. The rights of others must be respected.

- *Learn to manage conflicts.* Every relationship has some rough moments, but knowing what to do or say—and wanting to keep that friendship—is important.

3. Another point to bring out is that children express more positive feelings about other children who rely less on their teachers. This is not to say that there must be no contact with teachers, but children seem to resent other children who are constantly seeking contact with and approval from teachers. In other words, being a "brown-nose" or "teacher's pet" will probably not endear a child to his or her peers.

4. Once all of these have been discussed, it may be beneficial to do some more role playing. Some situations that may work well are:

- Two children are working on projects in a crafts club. Show how a conversation, and possibly a friendship, might start.

- Several children are hanging out or playing together. A new child enters the situation. Show a child using a cautious approach and then a direct approach to gain entry into the group. Then act out a child coming on too strong.

- A child discovers that others in the group are upset with his friend because he (choose any or all) has unhygienic habits, is too loud and self-centered, or has been accused of stealing something. Show how the child tactfully discusses this with his friend.

- Two students are friends but are having a conflict over (choose any or all) whose house to go to, both being interested in the same boy or girl, trying to make peace after a bad argument, or whether to admit to something they have just done that was wrong.

5. From here go on to developing confidants. Have the students go back to Activity 19-2 and complete the "My Friends" section. If anyone complains that the list would be endless, have them include only those who they feel are good friends. If they still can't pare the list down, make it only those with whom they have contact at least several times a week. Then have the children put a star next to only those names in whom they would confide. If the children are not sure how to delineate this, suggest that only names be included if they would tell this person that they had just won an award, committed a crime, been jilted by a boyfriend or girlfriend, or other sensitive information. To this list they should now add any other people in whom they would confide, such as clergy, relatives, or other acquaintances.

6. Follow with a discussion of what makes someone a good confidant. The importance of having someone else to share in your problems should be emphasized.

Follow-up Suggestion

Have the children add to their list of friends throughout the year and tell how they met and became friends.

Making Friends

DIRECTIONS: Complete the following lists.

Things I Look for in a Friend

_____

_____

_____

_____

_____

_____

_____

_____

_____

Things That Could Happen to End a Friendship

_____

_____

_____

_____

_____

_____

_____

_____

Name _____

Date _____

My Friends

DIRECTIONS: Complete the following lists.

Situations and Places Where I Have Met a New Friend

_____

_____

_____

_____

_____

_____

_____

_____

_____

_____

My Friends

_____

_____

_____

_____

_____

_____

_____

_____

LESSON 20

Creative Problem Solving

BACKGROUND FOR THE TEACHER

It is important to look at all sides of a situation and try different strategies until one is found to be successful. Many people, however, use a "tunnel-vision" approach, whereby they try one way and continue with it even when it doesn't work. Stress comes not only from the failure, but also from the frustration of feeling that the problem is unsolvable.

LESSON 20

Purpose: To show children that most problems have more than one possible solution so that they may begin to search for alternative solutions to the problems in their lives.

Materials Needed

Workbook Activities 20-1, 20-2 and 20-3

Directions

1. Have the children turn to Activity 20-1 in their workbooks. These exercises demonstrate that there are often several ways of looking at things and that there may be alternative solutions to a problem.

2. Have the children continue on to Activity 20-2 in their workbooks.

3. Now that the children realize that several solutions are possible, have them write their solutions to the problem situations found in Activity 20-3. Then discuss the children's answers together as a class. Alternative solutions will be offered by different children, and the class should begin to realize that several of them might work out.

Follow-up Suggestion

As an ongoing exercise, let the children use problem-solving techniques to help solve the many problem situations (such as fights, arguments, and so on) that occur in class. The children involved in each situation may even be asked for several possible solutions. Be sure that the situation, its problem aspects, and the outcome that each party would like are clear.

Answers to Activity 20-2

1. REDS to RIDS to BIDS to KIDS to KISS

2. MATS to MARS to MARE to MORE (or) EARS to MARS to MARE to MORE

3. SOOT to BOOT to BOON to BORN to BARN to YARN (or) SORT to SORE to BORE to BORN to BARN to YARN

4. LOOT to LOST to LOSE to POSE (or) LOOT to LOST to POST to POSE

5. CANS to CONS to CONE to COVE to MOVE (or) VAN to MANE to MARE to MORE to MOVE

Date _____

Looking at All Sides of a Problem

DIRECTIONS: Answer the following questions.

1. Which line between the points of the arrows is longer?

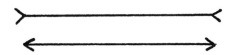

2. Which line is longer?

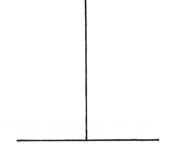

3. What do you see in this figure?

4. Is the book opening toward you or away from you?

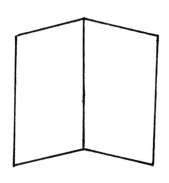

5. Which side looks nearest to you?

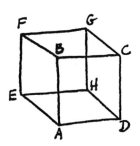

6. What kind of woman do you see here?

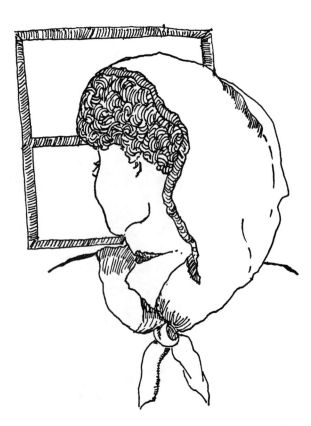

Changelings

DIRECTIONS: The following words can be changed from the first to the second by changing one letter at a time so that it always makes a new word. There are several ways that each could be changed. Here is an example of how one could be done:

change TINY to BIRD in four moves
(solution) TINY—TINS—BINS—BIND—BIRD

Now try these:

1. Change WEDS to KISS in four moves.

_____

_____

2. Change EATS to MORE in four moves.

_____

_____

3. Change SOFT to YARN in six moves.

_____

_____

4. Change LOOK to POSE in four moves.

_____

_____

5. Change VANS to MOVE in five moves.

_____

_____

What Would You Do?

DIRECTIONS: Write what you would do in the following situations.

1. Two girls who are friends both see the same boy at a dance and like him. He asks them both to dance, takes both phone numbers, and calls both to ask them out. What do you think each girl should do?

_____

_____

2. The teacher notices that two children have identical errors on a test and the identical grade. They sit right next to each other. What do you think the teacher should do?

_____

_____

3. There is a big, tough boy who is forcing five younger children to give him money each day. What do you think the younger children should do?

_____

_____

4. A boy had been "cutting up" in a certain class at the beginning of the year. Now he has stopped and is trying to do well, but the teacher obviously has it in for him and is picking on him. What do you think the boy should do?

_____

_____

5. The children in a class want to have a party. How do you think they should go about getting one during class time?

_____

_____

LESSON 21

Expressing Emotions

BACKGROUND FOR THE TEACHER

Releasing emotions reduces a person's stress. Letting another person know how you feel also helps to build stronger relationships in most cases.

LESSON 21

Purpose: To allow the children to assess the extent to which they express their emotions and to encourage the children to express them more.

Materials Needed

Workbook Activities 21-1 and 21-2

Directions

1. Read the following passage to the children:

Everybody has emotions. Expressing and sharing your positive emotions can bring great pleasure to you and to the others with whom you share them. Everybody likes to hear nice things about themselves. Do you tell people you like that you *do* like them? When someone does something to make you happy, do you tell that person that he or she made you happy? Holding in emotions can lead to stress. You need an outlet for expressing your displeasures so you can correct problem situations that led to it. If somebody does something to upset you, do you tell that person that you are upset or do you hold it in? If you let it out, you can release some of your bad feelings. You may also be able to prevent the person from doing it again. If the person doesn't know that he or she upset you, that person probably will do the same thing again.

2. Now ask the children if they know what upsets *you,* the teacher. Ask them how you express it to let them know.

3. Elicit from the children a list of possible emotions and record them on the chalkboard.

4. Have the children turn to Activity 21-1 in their workbooks and ask them to answer the questions.

5. Discuss the children's answers. Here are some examples:

- For question 1, things to say would be "I love you," "I like you," "I care," "You're nice (wonderful, great)," "I'm happy to see you," and "I was thinking about you."

- For question 2, things to do would be shake hands, pat the other person's back, touch a shoulder, kiss, look the other person in the eye and smile, and give the person a gift.

For questions 7 and 8, ask the children to put an *X* next to the emotion if he or she told the person to whom the emotion applied and *Y* if the child told a third person that he or she had felt that way.

6. Have the children complete the chart on Activity 21-2 in their workbooks and see how many emotions they have felt and may or may not have expressed.

Follow-up Suggestion

Ask the children to tell two people during the next week when they are feeling something good about the two people and when they are upset. It is better if this is done with people who are not in the same class, but this is not critical. Have a class discussion one week later about the positive and negative results of having expressed emotions. Let the children explain what happened.

Name _____

Date _____

Expressing Emotions

DIRECTIONS: Complete the following statements.

1. To let someone know I like him or her, some things I would *say* are:

_____

_____

2. To show someone I like him or her, some things I would *do* are:

_____

_____

3. In the last day I have *felt* the following emotions:

_____

_____

4. In the last week I have *felt* the following emotions:

__ _____

_____

5. In the last month I have *felt* the following emotions:

_____

_____

6. Now underline each of the above emotions that you have *told* to the person that you felt the emotion about. For example, if you wrote that in the last day you felt anger *and* you also told the person you were angry at that you were angry, underline the word anger.

Name _____

Date _____

7. In the last day I have *told* someone that I felt the following emotions:

_____

_____

8. In the last week I have *told* someone that I felt the following emotions:

_____

_____

9. In the last month I have *told* someone that I felt the following emotions:

_____

_____

10. Complete the chart in Activity 21-2.

Name _____   ACTIVITY 21–2

Date _____

Emotions Chart

DIRECTIONS: List your relatives (parents, grandparents, sisters, brothers, cousins, and such). Next to each name write an emotion (or more than one emotion) that you *feel* toward this person and write down the last time you *told* that person that you felt this emotion for him or her. You may also add friends or other people you know to the list.

Person's Name	Emotions I Feel	When I Last Told the Person My Emotions

Have you listed many emotions for each person or only one? You probably feel several emotions for each person. Have you told these people how you feel about them?

THURSDAY . . .

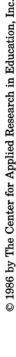

LESSON 22

Improving Self-Esteem

BACKGROUND FOR THE TEACHER

When people feel good about themselves, they are better able to handle stress. Self-image is evident in the way that people move, walk, speak, and generally present themselves to others. If people act like losers, others will react to them in that manner. The other extreme, that of being loud, bragging, and pushy, may also be a result of poor self-image.

This lesson is a good way to start the children off on emphasizing the positive. You can follow it up with a discussion of the benefits of thinking positively and carrying oneself well.

LESSON 22

Purpose: To accent the positive and to help the children begin to develop a positive self-image.

Materials Needed

Workbook Activities 22-1 and 22-2
Construction paper and marking pens

Directions

1. Begin a short discussion of how people sometimes rate others. The children will know that some children are known to be especially good-looking, smart, funny, and so on. They may even have some anecdotal stories of how ratings of one to ten have been given to children, usually based on looks. Direct the discussion to the fact that there are many things upon which to judge a person.

2. Have the children turn to Activity 22-1 in their workbooks and look at Part One. They are to rate themselves from one to ten.

3. Now have the children fill in Part Two. They must write down *at least ten* good things about themselves on the first chart. Then, for each child, select two other children to fill in the second chart with ten good things about the assigned child. Each child will now have his or her own list plus those of two other children listing good things about him or her. Give each child a piece of construction paper on which to put his or her name and the heading "Good Things About Me." They may put all of the selected traits from their lists and then decorate it.

4. Display the students' papers. Some wise-cracking and put-downs may occur, so be sure to step in and remind everyone that we are emphasizing the *positive.*

Follow-up Suggestion

Have the children fill in the chart on Activity 22-2 in their workbooks. Then have the children write, in the space provided, how they could improve the rating they gave themselves at the beginning of the lesson.

Name _____

Date _____

Feeling Good About Myself

DIRECTIONS FOR PART ONE: I would give myself a rating of (circle one)

1   2   3   4   5   6   7   8   9   10

DIRECTIONS FOR PART TWO: Fill in the following chart. Be sure to include at least ten good things about yourself.

Good Things About Me

_____

_____

_____

_____

_____

_____

Now have two other people fill in the following chart about you.

GOOD THINGS ABOUT_____   GOOD THINGS ABOUT_____

_____   _____

_____   _____

_____   _____

_____   _____

_____   _____

_____   _____

_____   _____

Me

DIRECTIONS: Rate yourself in each of the following areas. Circle the number on each scale that fits you:

looks	1	2	3	4	5	6	7	8	9	10
neatness	1	2	3	4	5	6	7	8	9	10
clothes	1	2	3	4	5	6	7	8	9	10
sense of humor	1	2	3	4	5	6	7	8	9	10
friendliness	1	2	3	4	5	6	7	8	9	10
concern for others	1	2	3	4	5	6	7	8	9	10
popularity	1	2	3	4	5	6	7	8	9	10
intelligence	1	2	3	4	5	6	7	8	9	10

How might you improve the rating you gave yourself in Part One of Activity 22–1?

_____

_____

_____

_____

_____

_____

_____

_____

_____

_____

Developing Coping Phrases

BACKGROUND FOR THE TEACHER

When you are in a stressful situation, it can help to repeat a positive phrase or statement to yourself in order to help you get through that situation. These positive statements are a way to cope.

LESSON 23

Purpose: To give the children practice in developing phrases that they can say to themselves to help them cope with specific stresses.

Materials Needed

Workbook Activity 23-1

Directions

Have the children turn to Activity 23-1 in their workbooks. They are to read the brief paragraph and then answer the questions. Tell the children not to just say that they know they are about to get upset. If they can, they should include in their statements how they will solve the problem. Be sure they use positive words, such as "I can" and "I will."

Follow-up Suggestion

Have the children try to actually use their coping statements when a stressor is present at home, in school, or on the playground. Later, discuss what happened.

My Coping Phrases

It can be helpful to develop statements that you repeat to yourself in stressful situations to remind yourself that you need not be suffering so much stress. If you practice the statements *before* going into the situation, you may be able to help yourself deal with the situation when it happens by repeating the statements to yourself. For example, maybe you know that you get embarrassed easily and suffer stress in many situations as a result. So, in an embarrassing situation, you can repeat to yourself, "I'm going to feel sure of myself and I know I'll do the right thing."

DIRECTIONS: Choose about five of the stressors that you checked off on the Stress Checklist in Activity 2–3. On the back of this sheet write a statement for each one that you might repeat to yourself to help you deal with the stressor a little better.

For example, if you had checked off that you get nervous trying out for things, you might make up a statement such as, "I'm a good baseball player. I know that. I'll relax and do my best." Be sure not to use negative words. Do not use "I'll try," "maybe," or "probably." Use positive words like "I will" and "I can."

LESSON 24

Nutrition

BACKGROUND FOR THE TEACHER

One thing that many people neglect to consider is nutrition. What you eat and the manner in which you eat it can be stressful. A change in either may affect how you feel and how susceptible to stress you become. Nutrition is a two-way street. Failure to get or use the nutrients that the body needs can prevent proper functioning of the body and can put strain on the system. On the other hand, stress may lead to improper body functioning, which then prevents the proper use of the nutrients.

One immediate concern should be how fast you eat. A person under stress tends to do things quickly, including eating. Since digestion begins in the mouth, with the chewing of food and mixing it with saliva and its digestive juices, eating quickly without chewing your food thoroughly can hinder the absorption of some nutrients. The system may also be strained if you eat while doing other activities. You really should sit down for a meal, eat slowly, chew your food thoroughly, and concentrate on eating instead of doing other things at the same time, such as reading or watching TV. A different, and also poor, reaction to stress is possible—some people simply stop eating.

Eating can be a problem in another way when psychological problems lead to unnecessary eating. This can, of course, lead to unhealthy obesity and can add the additional problem of anxiety about eating. A lowering of self-esteem, such as disappointment in one's lack of self-control, is also possible.

The following six classes of nutrients sustain the body by aiding growth, controlling the internal processes of the body, converting food into usable energy, and maintaining the body's temperature and chemical balance:

• *Water* is the main component of blood, sweat, urine, and all cells. We need about six 8-ounce glasses of fluid a day, some of which comes from food.

• Most of our energy comes from *carbohydrates* (sugar, honey, molasses, and starchy foods such as bananas, bread, cereal, grain, flour, milk, fruits, and vegetables). This is why people have been known to load up on carbohydrates before such heavy exercise as running a marathon. Carbohydrates also help us to utilize protein and fat.

• *Fats* (margarine, butter, cream, egg yolks, whole milk, avocados, ice cream, cheese, vegetable oil, salad dressing and mayonnaise) allow proteins to be used for building up cells instead of being burned for energy. They also carry fat-soluble vitamins and needed fatty acids.

Fats have had some association with heart disease, so it may be advisable to limit their intake. One to two tablespoons daily of polyunsaturated fatty acids are necessary and can be obtained from corn, safflower, cottonseed or soybean oil. You should limit foods that are high in cholesterol and saturated fat (cream cheese, sweet and sour cream, sausage, bacon, pork, lard, fatback, butter, hydrogenated margarine, and shortening).

• *Protein* (fish, poultry, lean meat, milk and milk products excluding butter, cream and cream cheese, egg whites, nuts, whole-grain products, legumes, and peanut butter) is important for building cells and tissues and is needed for energy. Excess protein is stored as fat.

• *Minerals.* Sodium, potassium, and chloride are needed to maintain our fluid balance. Sodium is mostly found in salt (which may also have harmful effects on blood pressure). It is also found in meat, cheese, milk, shellfish, poultry, fish, eggs, grains, and most processed foods. Calcium is necessary for our bones and teeth and is obtained from milk and milk products, green vegetables, salmon, sardines and bean curd. Phosphorus is also needed for our bodies and teeth and comes from milk and milk products. Iron is necessary because it combines with protein for the hemoglobin (which carries oxygen to tissues) in our blood. Two or three servings a day of iron-rich foods are recommended. A dilemma for some people is that many foods that are high in iron are also high in cholesterol (liver, kidneys, heart, liverwurst, and eggs). Lower cholesterol sources of iron are lean beef, dried beans, lentils, nuts, whole-grain products, prunes, apricots, bananas, veal, poultry, tuna, sardines, dried fruit, dark leafy vegetables, peanuts, and a number of other vegetables. *NOTE:* Tannic acid, found in tea, interferes with our utilization of iron.

Other minerals that are needed are iodine (found in iodized salt and some seafood), magnesium, zinc, chromium, copper, fluoride, manganese, selenium, and molybdenum.

• *Vitamins* act on nutrients and are found in almost all foods except sugar. An important point is that since vitamins *act on* nutrients, you cannot take vitamins *instead of* eating food, since you will not have the nutrients on which they are to act.

Vitamin A is important for skin and vision (adjusting from light to dark) and is supplied by green, leafy, and yellow-orange vegetables, deeply colored fruit, liver, egg yolks, milk, margarine, and butter.

The B-complex is made up of eleven vitamins and work best when taken together. They include: thiamin (B_1), riboflavin (B_2), niacin (B_3), pyridoxine (B_6), biotin, folic acid, cobolamine (B_{12}), para-amino-benzoic acid (PABA), inositol, choline, pantothenic acid. B vitamins are necessary for nervous system function, providing energy, and maintaining healthy skin, hair, and eyes.

Vitamin C helps the body to heal wounds and, although there is disagreement on this, has been claimed to help the body to resist disease. Whether or not you agree that large doses are helpful, at least one serving of vitamin-C rich food is necessary every day. Citrus fruits and certain vegetables are major sources of vitamin C.

Vitamin D helps us to utilize calcium and phosphorus and helps to build bones and teeth. We get vitamin D from fortified milk, fish-liver oils, certain fish (tuna, herring, salmon, mackerel), and from the sun acting on our skin.

Vitamin E is necessary for our body's preservation of some vitamins and unsaturated fatty acids and for cell growth. Margarine, whole grain bread, cereal grains, and vegetable and seed oils are sources of vitamin E.

Vitamin K is necessary for the clotting of blood and is obtained from green, leafy vegetables and, to a lesser extent, from cereals, fruits, dairy products, and meat.

• *Fiber* is the part of the food which is not digested by the body. It is essential for normal functioning of the intestinal tract. Recent studies have shown the importance of a high fiber diet in helping to reduce the possibilities of colon cancer and heart disease. Fruits, especially apple skins, vegetables, bran, and other whole grains are good sources of fiber.

The government established recommended daily allowances for each of these classes of nutrients years ago. All requirements are affected by age, body size, stage of growth, sex, and activity levels.

Many so-called "junk foods" supply calories, but very little in the way of nutrients. The body uses nutrients that have been stored up as it metabolizes these foods, but the nutrients are not replaced by the junk food. You then gain calories but lose nutrients. Processed foods and foods that are overrefined may fall into this class of foods as well. Some empty calorie foods are sweets, soft drinks, potato chips, and pretzels. An obvious problem with eating junk foods is that the person may then not have any appetite left for eating nutritious food. Try to substitute healthier snacks (fruits, nuts, cooked or raw vegetables, cheese, milk, unsweetened juices and drinks, dry unsugared cereal, plain yogurt with sliced fruit, and unsalted popcorn) for junk food.

Some substances can actually simulate a stress-type response in the body. Sugar and caffeine fall into this category. These are potentially harmful for many people, especially if they are consumed in large amounts. The effects of caffeine, for example, very closely mirror the body's responses in a stress reaction. Caffeine also acts as a diuretic, flushing out some vitamins. This depletes the body of needed nutrients. The combination of caffeine and refined sugar puts even more strain on the body. Caffeine is found in coffee, as most people know, but is also in tea, chocolate, and many colas.

It is often obvious which foods and beverages contain sugar. Most breakfast cereals, for example, list sugar as a main ingredient. Sugar is also in canned fruits and vegetables, jams and jellies, peanut butter, TV dinners, catsup, salad dressings, tomato sauce, and many other foods. Read the ingredients of the foods you eat for a week. They are generally listed in the order of their concentration in the product. See how many of the foods you eat list sugar as one of the first few ingredients and how many others list it as a less important ingredient. Be aware of the other names for sugar as well, including dextrose, fructose, and sucrose. You can get all the sugar your body needs for energy from the complex carbohydrates contained in fresh fruits and vegetables, bread, grains, and potatoes. The body has no need for refined sugar, and it can be harmful. It can cause cavities and may even result in diabetes and hypoglycemia. Be aware also that using honey as a substitute will still elevate your blood sugar level. Even if you find it impossible to drastically cut down on sugar, you can cut down gradually. Put a little less in your coffee or on your cereal. Eat shredded wheat or bran flakes without sugar at breakfast. Start getting used to the taste of things without sugar. In time, you probably won't even miss it!

Several other points should be made here. When cooking food, you affect its nutritional value as well. When boiling vegetables, for example, you should use water that is already boiling so that the cooking time is reduced and more vitamins are kept in. Covering the pot and not stirring also helps to keep in vitamins and minerals. Vegetables should be cooked until tender but still firm. An even better way to preserve nutrients is to stir fry vegetables in only a little liquid or vegetable oil, keep the pan covered, and cook only for a short time. In steaming, use about one inch of water and a steamer tray, keep it covered, and cook to a crisp consistency.

Another very important point is that almost everyone needs to eat breakfast. However, loading up on caffeine and sugar is not the way to start the day. Cereal, juice, whole-grain muffins or bread, milk, yogurt, a banana or other fruit, an egg (not too often), and even peanut or nut (almond, cashew) butter are much better ways to start the day than donuts and coffee.

A few more points may be made regarding nutrition. One is that salt intake may need to be limited due to possible detrimental effects on the heart and blood pressure. A second is that it is possible to be allergic to certain foods. Restlessness, dizziness, headaches, sleeplessness, digestive and respiratory problems, and disorientation may result. Milk and milk products, wheat and corn are common culprits. Another important consideration is the effect of alcohol, particularly on the liver. Alcohol causes several parts of the body (liver, pancreas, and kidney) to work harder and has very little nutritional value, while being high in calories. It also may deplete needed vitamins and can be a problem regarding blood sugar. Although many people drink alcohol because they believe it helps them relieve stress, it really only depresses the nervous system temporarily, blocking some responses and doing nothing about the real problems. Drugs, too, are substances introduced into the body that may have harmful short- and long-term effects. Smoking has, of course, also been found to be hazardous to health.

Nutrition could not be discussed without a word about chemical additives. The reasons that they are added to food are generally for appearance, flavor, and to prevent spoilage. The long-term effects are not certain, however, and there have been some indications that some may be carcinogenic (cancer-causing). Some additives may cause immediate reactions in some people. Monosodium glutamate (MSG), for example, has been known to cause headaches and dizziness. Additives to avoid are sodium nitrate, sodium nitrite, BHT, MSG, and saccharin.

In general it is best to make your diet as "natural" as possible. Natural or whole foods have no part removed and have not been chemically altered. You might follow the philosophy of "when in doubt, leave it out." Each person must make a decision as to what he or she will put into his or her body. This decision should at least be made after careful researching.

LESSON 24

Purpose: To educate the children on some of the facts about good nutrition and to emphasize its importance.

Materials Needed

Workbook Activities 24-1 and 24-2

Directions

1. Ask the children to tell you what they ate so far today. Record on the chalkboard as many different foods as are mentioned and that you can write down in a few minutes. Keep them in separate columns entitled "Breakfast," "Lunch," and "Snacks." Have the children tell you in which column each food belongs.

2. After several minutes, stop and have everyone look the chart over. Decide which foods are "junk foods" and which have sugar. Put a "J" next to the junk foods and an "S" after foods containing sugar. Have everyone note how many foods have these letters next to them.

3. Now have the children turn to Activity 24-1 in their workbooks and list all the foods they have eaten in the last 24 hours.

4. Discuss material from the background section.

5. After you have presented the material, direct the children to keep track of all foods they eat for the next week and to add this information to the list in Activity 24-1.

Follow-up Suggestions

1. Have the children turn to Activity 24-2 and add up the calories they've consumed in any one day. You will have to bring in a calorie-counter wheel or a book containing caloric information.

2. Have the children take turns bringing in a food they eat to which the other children may not have been exposed. This can be done as reports, demonstrations or even tastings.

3. Analyze the school lunch menu as to calories, nutritional components, and so on.

4. Ask the children to help in the preparation of food at home and to report back to the class.

5. Assign reports for extra credit on the government's Recommended Daily Allowances (RDA); the pros and cons of chemical additives (this could also be a debate); and what "enriched food" is.

6. Ask the children to report back on any startling discoveries they made when reading the labels of foods.

7. Ask the children to look up the ingredients in everything in one of their meals. In an advanced group, you might have the students research what all the ingredients (particularly long chemical names) actually mean.

Diet Diary

Foods I Have Eaten in the Last 24 Hours

_____

_____

_____

_____

_____

_____

_____

_____

_____

_____

_____

Foods I Have Eaten in the Last Week

_____

_____

_____

_____

_____

_____

_____

_____

_____

_____

_____

Name _____

Date _____

Calorie Counter

DIRECTIONS: Add up the calories in the foods you have eaten in one day.

FOOD	AMOUNT EATEN	CALORIES

LESSON 25

Leisure-Time Activities

BACKGROUND FOR THE TEACHER

Leisure-time activities can serve as a break from stressful pursuits and situations. Included in these leisure-time activities is exercise, which was discussed in Lesson 7.

LESSON 25

Purpose: To show the children the many alternatives that may be chosen as leisure-time activities.

Materials Needed

Product of a hobby or materials and tools used in a hobby

Workbook Activity 25-1

Directions

1. Tell the children about a hobby of yours. If possible, bring in something to illustrate it, such as a finished product or the materials and tools used for it. Tell about when you get a chance to pursue your hobby and what you get out of it. You can do the same with a sport that you play, particularly if it is one with which the children are not likely to be familiar.

Be sure to mention that it is important to leave yourself time for hobbies, sports, and leisure-time activities. (You can call it "play time" for younger children.)

2. Have the children turn to Activity 25-1 in their workbooks and fill in the chart.

3. Discuss any hobbies with which the children are unfamiliar.

4. Let the children tell about their hobbies.

Follow-up Suggestion

Let the children demonstrate their hobbies.

Leisure-Time Activities Checklist

DIRECTIONS: Place an *X* next to each activity you do. Place a *T* next to each one that sounds as if it might be interesting to try.

COLLECTING

_____ dolls
_____ autographs
_____ bells
_____ stamps
_____ fossils
_____ coins
_____ buttons
_____ cans

_____ labels
_____ newspaper headlines
_____ match covers
_____ miniatures
_____ records
_____ postcards
_____ patches
_____ sports cards

_____ comics
_____ theater programs
_____ seashells
_____ rocks and minerals
_____ antiques
_____ buckles
_____ greeting cards

other_____

ARTS AND CRAFTS

_____ card making
_____ puppetry
_____ jewelry design
_____ basketry
_____ doll making
_____ pottery
_____ candlemaking
_____ weaving
_____ embroidery
_____ knitting

_____ crewel
_____ sewing
_____ woodworking/carpentry
_____ enameling
_____ leather craft
_____ stained glass
_____ collage
_____ mobiles
_____ sculpture
_____ glass blowing

_____ restoring antiques
_____ making fishing lures
_____ quilting
_____ mosaics
_____ carving
_____ making models
_____ papier-mâché
_____ painting
_____ painting by number
_____ photography

other_____

OTHER

_____ gardening
_____ reading
_____ printing
_____ cooking
_____ computer games

_____ raising fish or
　　　 other animals
_____ writing
_____ playing an instrument
_____ singing
_____ astronomy

_____ working with automobiles
_____ checkers, chess,
　　　 backgammon
_____ board games
_____ magic
_____ ham radio/CB

other_____

SPORTS

_____ baseball
_____ football
_____ basketball
_____ tennis
_____ soccer
_____ bowling

_____ table tennis
_____ hockey
_____ billiards
_____ swimming
_____ weight lifting
_____ racquetball

_____ running
_____ track and field
_____ wrestling
_____ boxing
_____ fencing
_____ fishing

other_____

LESSON 26

Biofeedback

BACKGROUND FOR THE TEACHER

Because biofeedback is a particularly promising field and is a technique that is highly successful in helping people to manage stress, a more detailed explanation is in order.

Through the years, stories had been filtering into the western world of yogis who were supposedly performing impossible feats. It was said that there were some who could stop their heart and perform other feats thought to be impossible. Heart rate was thought to be totally out of the realm of human control. It was common medical belief some 20 years ago that heart rate, blood pressure, skin temperature and skin resistance, and a number of other functions were controlled by the autonomic nervous system. *Autonomic* was seen as synonymous with *automatic*. That is, it was out of the realm of control. At that time, several scientific studies were performed. In these studies, yogis were examined and asked to exert control over these supposedly automatic functions. Measurements were taken to see if they could actually exercise control. Although it was not possible to get the highest-level yogis to participate in the experiment, it was discovered that the yogis tested were indeed able to exert control over these functions. Although none stopped his heart, they were able to slow their heart rate and change their metabolic rate, blood pressure, and brain waves. This, of course, led to a restructuring of beliefs as to what was and was not beyond a person's control.

Scientists realized that these yogis had spent years studying their internal responses and finding the techniques needed to produce changes. It was also realized that few people in western society had the time or the discipline to do the same. We did have one thing that the yogis did not have, however, and that was technology. There existed machines that could measure the responses of the body. What was needed was a way of enabling the person to get the information. The solution to the problem was to modify the equipment so that it not only measured the responses of the body constantly, but also "fed back" information on what was occurring to the person being measured. This was the beginning of the term "biofeedback." There was feedback being given as to the functioning of the body. It was discovered that when a person was getting information on the second-by-second changes in a function, he or she was found to be able to control it by hooking in to the response and exerting control over it. The key was the information that was now available to him or her. For example, hand temperature is a dynamic, or constantly changing, function. The temperature (actually a measure of blood flow) is constantly going up and down. Normally you have no awareness of the minute changes. However, by using a machine that tells you, through changes in lights or sounds, exactly when it goes up and down, you can learn how to control your hand temperature.

At first this seemed to be simply an extremely interesting phenomenon from a research standpoint. It was discovered, however, that by training people to elicit changes in bodily processes, there were some clinical benefits. People suffering from headaches, who had been used in some of the studies, reported that they were getting relief from the headaches as a side effect. It was discovered that training people to decrease the activity of the frontalis muscles of the forehead and to increase hand temperature seemed to help headache sufferers. Several other clinical uses became immediately apparent. If a person suffered from Raynaud's disease, for example, and had problems with blood circulation to the hand, it made sense to train him or her to control the circulation of the blood to the hand. In later years it was discovered that by giving feedback on different bodily functions, a number of problems could be successfully dealt with. Asthma, stress-induced eczyma, bruxism (grinding the teeth), subvocalization during reading, stuttering, tics, and pain have all been treated successfully. Biofeedback has been used as a relaxation training tool and has been used in treating general and specific anxieties and phobias. Hyperactivity in children has also been treated successfully. Biofeedback techniques have been used in treating with-drawing alcoholics, and there have been promising results in neuromuscular reeducation and the treatment of paralysis, Bell's palsy, foot drop, phantom limb pain, spasmodic torticollis, temperomandibular joint syndrome, blepharospasm, fecal incontinence, peptic ulcers, irritable bowel syndrome, cardiovascular disorders, hypertension, epilepsy, and general stress.

The principle in all cases is the same: By giving a person information on what is happening in his or her body, the person is able to hook in to the response and exert control. It is the same with regard to stress-related problems. A person has been responding to stress by having physiological changes occur. These are a result of his or her own reaction to the stress. Since it is the person's own reaction, he or she is able to hook in to what has been going on within him- or herself (through the aid of the equipment) and then regain control. For example, if Carol wants to learn to relax, she can learn to lower her body's physical arousal level by getting information on its functioning and learning to produce changes. If Carol is also experiencing facial tics, she would learn to hook in to the muscle activity of the affected area (the face, in this example) and control it. The equipment simply gives Carol the information that had been unavailable before on the minute muscle activity level changes.

Biofeedback should not be considered the miracle cure of the decade. When used in conjunction with other relaxation techniques and counseling techniques, however, it seems to hold great promise in dealing with a number of problems, including stress.

LESSON 26

Purpose: To introduce the children to the principle of biofeedback.

Materials Needed

Finger thermometers

Workbook Activity 26-1

Directions

1. Ask the children to sit still while they (a) slow down their heart rate, (b) make their hands warm, and (c) relax their forehead muscles. Remind the children that before they had begun doing relaxation exercises, they probably would have told you that they couldn't do any of these things. Now that they have learned these techniques, they may feel able to do them, particularly the latter two. They have learned, by concentrating, how to control some of the things that their bodies do.

2. Use the background material to describe the principles of biofeedback and how it developed. Be sure to tell the children that the word "biofeedback" has two parts: "bio" has to do with the body and "feedback" has to do with information about what is happening. You can point out that learning to walk, write, play sports, and ride a bicycle all have aspects of getting feedback on whether what we are doing with our bodies is correct.

3. Obtain finger thermometers for the students. These are available from:

J & J Products
22797 Holgar Court NE
Poulsbo, WA 98370
(206) 779-3853

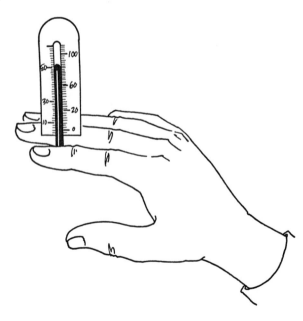

Have the children measure their finger temperature at different times. They do this by holding the thermometer between the second and third fingers as shown in the illustration. They can then measure the temperature before, during, and after their relaxation exercises.

4. Have the children turn to Activity 26-1 in their workbooks. By keeping a record over a period of time, the children can see how they really can control their bodies. (As the children relax, the hand temperature should rise.)

Follow-up Suggestions

1. Have the children continue to record their hand temperatures on the chart.

2. If possible, ask a local professional to bring in and demonstrate his or her biofeedback equipment.

Biofeedback Chart of Hand Temperature

DIRECTIONS: Use the following chart to keep a record of your hand temperature at certain times. By doing this, you can see how you really can control your body.

Day	Time	Activity	Hand Temperature (note if taken before, during, or after activity)

LESSON 27

Healing Practices

BACKGROUND FOR THE TEACHER

Here are brief summaries of a number of healing professions and practices and what they claim to do.

Physical Health

Physicians (M.D.). You have probably all seen a doctor and know all about how he or she examines you, diagnoses your problem, and prescribes medication if necessary. At times, the physician even operates to correct a condition.

Dentists (D.D.S.). You are probably all familiar with dentists, also. They examine your teeth, clean them, and, if there is decay, fill them. Dental specialists also straighten teeth (orthodontists), work on gums (periodontists), and perform oral surgery (oral surgeons).

Osteopaths (D.O.). Osteopathy is a healing practice that believes many physical problems are the result of structural abnormalities. Practitioners use physical manipulation of bones and muscles, drug therapy, and surgery.

Holistic Physicians. This refers to persons using an approach that treats the entire person rather than a symptom. It combines traditional medical practices with stress reduction, diet, and exercise. It emphasizes the person's role in maintaining good health.

Chiropractors. These professionals treat physical and structural problems by manipulating the bones, especially the spine.

Homeopathic Doctors. These are holistic practitioners who use very low doses of medicine to balance the body and increase resistance.

Mental Health

Psychoanalysts. Deal with psychoanalysis, developed by Sigmund Freud, a method of treating abnormal behavior. Psychoanalysis is usually long-term therapy and analyzes early development, family relations, and unconscious behavior. Analysts may have a medical background and often use drugs as part of therapy.

Psychologists and Psychotherapists. Treat emotional and mental problems with various therapeutic techniques. Today it is difficult to determine what is normal or abnormal behavior, and many healthy people seek therapy in order to learn how to handle the many emotional problems that occur in their lives.

Gestalt Therapists. Help so-called "normal" individuals to better develop their personalities in order to live fuller lives. Combines eastern and western aspects of psychology.

Reichian Therapists. Use method developed by psychoanalyst Wilhelm Reich, who believed in treating both the physical and mental symptoms. Therapists use analytic techniques and physical exercises.

Bio-energetics. This was developed by Alexander Lowen, a student of Reich's. He furthered Reich's concepts by adding more physical components, such as breathing, massage, and releasing exercises.

Relaxation Techniques

These all seek to engage the relaxation response.

Autogenic Training. This calms the autonomic nervous system by using images of physical sensations that are associated with relaxation. The individual repeats such phrases as "My arms and legs are heavy and warm."

Hypnosis. This is a practice of putting a person into a deep, relaxed state through suggestion, and then introducing positive statements that are easily accepted by the mind.

Jacobsen's Progressive Relaxation. This is a systematic contracting and releasing of muscle groups throughout the body in order to release muscle tension.

Biofeedback. This is a process of obtaining information about a specific physiological function in order to learn to control it. Biofeedback instruments monitor, amplify, and feed back to the patient his or her brain waves, heart rate, temperature, and muscle tension.

Meditation. Although considered by many to be a spiritual activity, meditation has been found to induce the relaxation response. The meditating individual focuses his or her attention completely on one object, word, or thought. Meditation methods common in the United States are Zen and transcendental meditation (TM).

Movement Awareness Techniques

These increase physical and mental awareness and improve movement behavior by changing poor muscle habits.

Alexander Technique. This is a one-on-one situation. The teacher gently guides the student physically through various positions, sitting, and walking, while asking the student to "inhibit" any response and to let the teacher show a better one.

Feldenkrais Technique. Takes two forms: Awareness Through Movement classes offer verbal instruction in various exercises aimed at improving the integration of movement patterns and of proper nervous system responses. Functional integration is a one-on-one situation that uses gentle physical manipulation to integrate the body.

Ideokinesis. This does not use actual physical movement, but rather has the student visualize images that help to achieve desired body patterns.

Kinetic Awareness. This teaches the individual to move each body part in all the directions it will go, slowly and with little effort, while becoming aware of what the body really feels like at all times. This exercise uses a soft rubber ball under body parts to gently massage the area.

Body Therapies

These include:

- **Reflexology**—finger stimulation of specific points located in the feet that are said to correspond with organs and parts of the body; often used in combination with massage or shiatzu.

- **Rolfing**—involves 10 one-hour sessions in which the connective tissue surrounding the muscles is physically manipulated; releases tension and helps align the body.

- **Massage**—manipulates muscles in order to release muscle tension, lactic acid buildup and increase circulation.

Eastern Practices

These include:

- **Oriental Medicine**—both preventive and curative. It emphasizes the body's natural powers to heal itself.

- **Acupuncture**—a method of healing that involves the insertion of needles into specific points on the skin, or meridians, which are channels of living magnetic energy in the body.

- **Auriculotherapy**—acupuncture on the ear, based on theory that the ear has points which correspond to organs and body parts.

- **Acupressure**—a Chinese massage technique that stimulates acupuncture points with the fingers or special devices.

- **Shiatzu**—a Chinese massage technique that seeks to balance the body by using strong finger pressure on specific points or meridians.

Physical Activity

Physical Exercise. This is any activity that works the body beyond its normal daily demands. Physical exercise helps the body to function more efficiently. Two types of physical exercise are:

- Yoga—an ancient method of physical exercise developed in India; it seeks to combine mind, body, and spirit through various slow physical positions, which help keep the body strong and flexible.
- Aerobics—refers to any activity that involves a sustained increase in oxygen consumption; it is important for physical fitness.

NOTE: This lesson is not meant to be an endorsement of these healing practices, but rather simply to mention what each claims to do. Many of these are part of a growing movement toward individuals taking the responsibility for and control of their own health.

LESSON 27

Purpose: To briefly introduce the children to the many kinds of healers to whom people turn for help.

Materials Needed

Workbook Activity 27-1

Directions

1. Choose several of the healers from the background material. Ask the children if any of them has ever gone to one for help or if they know anyone else who has. Ask if the children know what the healer did.

2. Have the children turn to Activity 27-1 in their workbooks. You may either use this as a research lesson and have the children use resources to discover what each does, or you may use the background material to tell the children what each does. The children can then fill in the spaces themselves. You don't have to go into great detail and you certainly don't have to endorse any of the methods. The purpose is simply to make the children aware that these methods exist and that there are people who say they have been helped by each.

Follow-up Suggestion

If possible, have the children interview several different types of practitioners, or ask several practitioners to visit the class and describe their healing practices.

Name _____

Date _____

Healing Practices

DIRECTIONS: Write a brief summary of what each does.

Physician _____

_____

_____

Dentist _____

_____

_____

Osteopath _____

_____

_____

Holistic Healer _____

_____

_____

Chiropractor _____

_____

_____

Homeopathic Doctor _____

_____

_____

Psychologist _____

_____

_____

Psychoanalyst _____

_____

_____

Psychotherapist _____

_____

_____

Gestalt Therapist _____

_____

_____

Reichian Therapist _____

_____

_____

Acupuncturist _____

_____

_____

Reflexologist _____

_____

_____

Rolfing Therapist _____

_____

_____

Masseuse _____

_____

_____

Yogi _____

_____

_____

Aerobic Instructor _____

_____

_____

LESSON 28

Desensitization

BACKGROUND FOR THE TEACHER

Desensitization has been used to help people overcome fears. It is a technique that can be incorporated into a person's own way of dealing with his or her individual stresses, anxieties, and fears.

LESSON 28

Purpose: To explain to the children how the technique called "desensitization" works.

Materials Needed

Workbook Activity 28-1

Directions

1. Keep a tally on the chalkboard as you ask the class how many children are afraid of snakes, dogs, insects, heights, closed spaces, flying, taking tests, and speaking in front of other people. Explain that these are common fears and that everyone has certain things that are upsetting to him or her.

2. Tell the children that there is a technique called "desensitization" that can help people overcome their fears. Now that they know some of the relaxation skills, they can try it.

3. Have the children turn to Activity 28-1 in their workbooks and read the explanation. If you have a fear and plan out a step-by-step desensitization procedure for yourself, share it with the children so that they can see how it is done.

Follow-up Suggestions

1. Go over the list of stressful situations from Lesson 2 or use any that the child feels appropriate. Have each child use the worksheet for Activity 28-1 in the workbook to plan how he or she could create five steps that would start out with only a slight relationship to the feared situation and would continue to approach it more closely.

2. Ideally, someone will use the technique in overcoming a fear. If so, have that child share the story with the others.

Desensitization

DIRECTIONS: Read the following information, then complete the worksheet.

This technique can be tried at any time, but it is even more powerful once the relaxation techniques taught in this program are learned. It is helpful to be adept enough to truly relax when you attempt to relax. The reason is that you are going to be trying to learn to relax while you are in contact with an unpleasant or stressful situation.

Take the example of Peter, who is afraid of snakes. The desensitization procedure may be something like this:

First, Peter does the relaxation exercises and gets into a relaxed state. Then he has contact with something related to snakes. This contact must start out as something very far removed from actual contact with snakes. He might simply hear the word "snakes" or see it written on a piece of paper. He must try to continue to relax. If Peter can't, he stops looking at the word and relaxes again. After a number of trials (or even sessions) Peter should be able to relax in the presence of this, as it is very far removed from the actual object of his fear.

The next step is for Peter to try to relax in the presence of something a little more closely related to the real object of fear, such as a magazine article about snakes. After learning to relax in the presence of this, a still more threatening stimulus is used, such as a picture of a snake. Each step may take some time before it can be successfully dealt with. The idea is for Peter to get closer and closer to the real thing in small steps that are easily handled. For Peter, future steps might be relaxing in the vicinity of the reptile house at the zoo, in the reptile house itself, in front of a snake display, and even possibly holding a harmless snake. Again, realize that this may take a long time.

The principle is, then, that you are relaxing in situations that start off far removed, but then get closer and closer to the real thing on which the fear is based. The technique can be used on other, less dramatic, fears also. Overcoming the fear of speaking in front of a group, another person, taking tests, and so on, is possible. By learning to relax in situations approximating the feared one, you may be able to relax in the situation itself.

Name _____

Date _____

Desensitizing My Fear of _____

DIRECTIONS: After your teacher has explained how desensitization works, plan out your own sequence. Choose a fear you have or a situation that upsets you. Decide on at least five steps that would get you closer to the real situation.

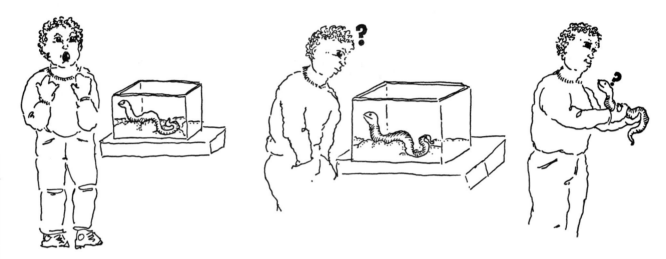

EXAMPLE: If you said you were afraid to fly in an airplane, you might do the following:

1. Learn to relax while looking at a picture of an airplane.
2. Learn to relax while talking to someone else about flying in an airplane.
3. Learn to relax while sitting in an airplane simulator.
4. Learn to relax while in an airport.
5. Learn to relax in a plane on the ground (knowing that it will not take off).
6. Learn to relax on a plane actually flying somewhere.

DIRECTIONS: Write your fear here:

My fear is _____

On the back of this sheet, write what steps you would take to desensitize yourself of this fear.

Bibliography

Alberti, Robert, and Michael L. Emmons. *Your Perfect Right: A Guide to Assertive Behavior,* 3rd ed. San Luis Obispo, California: Impact Publishers, 1974.

Benson, Herbert, and Miriam Z. Klipper. *The Relaxation Response.* New York: Avon Books, 1976.

Benson, Herbert. *The Mind/Body Effect.* New York: Berkley Books, 1980.

Bertherat, Therese, and Carol Bernstein, *The Body Has Its Reasons.* New York: Avon Books, 1979.

Carper, Jean. *The All-in-One Calorie Counter.* New York: Bantam Books, 1980.

Cooper, Cary L. *The Stress Check.* Englewood Cliffs, New Jersey: Prentice-Hall, 1981.

Cooper, Kenneth H. *Aerobics.* New York: M. Evans, 1968.

Cox, Tom. *Stress.* Baltimore, Maryland: University Park Press, 1978.

Dewey, John. *Human Nature and Conduct.* New York: Modern Library, 1965; reprint of 1922 edition.

Elkind, David. *The Hurried Child: Growing Up Too Fast Too Soon.* Reading, Massachusetts: Addison-Wesley, 1981.

_____ *All Grown Up and No Place to Go: Teenagers in Crisis.* Reading, Massachusetts: Addison-Wesley, 1984.

Feldenkrais, Moshe. *Awareness Through Movement.* New York: Harper & Row, 1972.

Friedman, Meyer, and Ray Rosenman. *Type A Behavior and Your Heart.* New York: Knopf, 1974.

Gelb, Michael. *Body Learning: The Alexander Technique.* New York: Deliah Books, 1981.

Jacobson, Edmund. *Progressive Relaxation.* Chicago: University of Chicago Press, 1974.

———— *You Must Relax.* New York: McGraw-Hill, 1978.

Kapit, Wynn, and Lawrence M. Elson. *The Anatomy Coloring Book.* New York: Harper & Row, 1977.

Lindsey, Ruth, Billie J. Jones, and Ada Van Whittley. *Body Mechanics: Posture Figure Fitness.* Dubuque, Iowa: William C. Brown, 1968.

Mason, L. John. *Guide to Stress Reduction.* Culver City, California: Peace Press, 1980.

Mirkin, Gabe, and Marshall Hoffman. *The Sports Medicine Book.* Boston: Little, Brown, 1978.

Norfolk, Donald. *The Stress Factor.* New York: Simon & Schuster, 1977.

Pelletier, Kenneth R. *Mind as Healer, Mind as Slayer.* New York: Dell, 1977.

Phillips, Beeman N. *School Stress and Anxiety.* New York: Human Sciences Press, 1978.

Powell, Robin. "Body Awareness: The Kinetic Awareness Work of Elaine Summers." Ph.D. diss., New York University, 1985.

Rosenman, R. H., M. Friedman, and R. Strauss. "A Predictive Study of Coronary Heart Disease," *Journal of The American Medical Association,* 189, 15–22, 1964.

Schultz, Edward W., and Charles M. Heuchert. *Child Stress and the School Experience.* New York: Human Sciences Press, 1983.

Schultz, Johannes, and Wolfgang Luthe, eds. *Autogenic Therapy.* New York: Grune & Stratton, 1969.

Selye, Hans. *Stress Without Distress.* New York: New American Library, 1976.

Speads, Carol H. *Breathing: The ABC's.* New York: Harper & Row, 1978.

Sweigard, Lulu E. *Human Movement Potential.* New York: Harper & Row, 1974.

Tavris, Carol. *Anger: The Misunderstood Emotion.* New York: Simon & Schuster, 1982.

Todd, Mabel Ellsworth. *The Thinking Body.* New York: Dance Horizons, 1972; reprint of the 1937 edition published by Paul B. Hoeber.

Walker, C. Eugene. *Learn to Relax.* Englewood Cliffs, New Jersey: Prentice-Hall, 1975.

Index